Dhamma Now 2

Sarah Procter Abbott

2025

Published in 2025 by:
Zolag
www.zolag.co.uk

ISBN 9781897633533
Copyright Sarah Procter Abbott

This work is licensed under the:
Creative Commons Attribution-NoDerivs 3.0 Unported License.
To view a copy of this license, visit:
http://creativecommons.org/licenses/by-nd/3.0/

Contents

	Preface	v
1	**May 2021**	1
	64 Helping Others	1
	65 Path to Enlightenment	2
	66 Vegetarian	3
	67 Suicide of Monks	4
	68 What is Practice?	6
	69 Accumulations	7
	70 Appears Well	9
2	**June 2021**	11
	71 The Seed and Fertiliser for the Path	11
	72 Letting Go	13
	73 Breath	15
	74 Unknown Defilements	16
	75 Khandha and Upādāna khandha	18
	76 Nothing, Something, Nothing	20
	77 The Point of Understanding	21
	78 A Moment	22
	79 Protection	24
	80 A Certain Person	25
	81 The Simple Life	26
	82 Trapped by the idea of Self	28
	83 Conceit	29

	84	The Signs & Details of Realities	30
3	**July 2021**		**33**
	85	How to Cultivate the Way	33
	86	Mettā to the Dead?	34
	87	The Truth is always the Truth	35
	88	Thira Saññā (Firm Remembrance)	36
	89	Pariyatti Understanding	37
	90	Understanding the Nimitta (signs)	38
	91	Inner and Outer Realities	40
	92	Don't Rush to Understand More!	41
	93	Saddhā makes Clear and Clean	43
	94	Foot of the World	44
	95	Deep	45
	96	The Good Guy	46
4	**August 2021**		**49**
	97	What is Hidden?	49
5	**November 2021**		**51**
	98	Tears	51
	99	Illumination of the Truth	53
	100	Dukkha	54
	101	Clear Understanding	55
6	**December 2021**		**57**
	102	The Masterpiece	57
	103	The Result of Kamma	59
	104	The End of Saṃsāra	60
	105	The 3 Gocaras (1)	62
	106	Āyūhana	63
	107	The 3 Gocaras (2)	65
	108	Anger	66
	109	Passing Away	68
	110	Wrong Practice	69

7 January 2022 — 73
- 111 Citta is Paṇḍara (pure) — 73
- 112 The Abhidhamma is Now — 75
- 113 Falling Down — 77

8 February 2022 — 79
- 114 Kamma and Birth — 79
- 115 Fire! (1) — 80

9 April 2022 — 83
- 116 Fire! (2) — 83
- 117 Kusala and Akusala Sīla — 85
- 118 Troubles in the World — 87
- 119 Forgetfulness — 89
- 120 Calm — 91
- 121 Sakkāya Diṭṭhi — 93
- 122 The Drunken Driver — 94
- 123 The Body — 96
- 124 Relax, it's Gone! — 98

Glossary — 100
Biography — 105
Further Study — 106

Preface

Ajahn Sujin Boriharnwanaket has encouraged me to share another set of my jottings (or summaries) of discussions by Zoom with friends around the world.

Those discussions were, as always, about the understanding of what is real, what is Dhamma now, as taught by the Buddha. Without careful consideration of the truths declared by the Buddha, as opposed to our usual assumptions of the way things are, there will never be an end to ignorance in life.

I have added a quote from the Buddhist scriptures to each jotting to show how the discussion relates to the original teachings of the Buddha.

With my great appreciation for the invaluable guidance given by Ajahn Sujin over many decades, I offer this book to assist readers with the development of understanding in daily life.

I also wish to acknowledge the great support and assistance of my husband Jonothan and the encouragement and help of the publisher, Alan Weller.

Sarah Procter Abbott

May 2021

64

Helping Others

There were discussions about how to help others. In particular, Jeff wondered how he could help prison inmates.

The best way to help others is to be a good friend with understanding. We can encourage others to do good and to develop wholesome mental states. We can be kind with compassion and help in a way the others find useful. When it is time, there can be talk about the Dhamma in daily life. This can condition thoughts about the truth. We can do our best to help others not to be hurt by their unwholesome mental states. What one is most hurt by are one's own defilements and bad deeds.

We cannot make fixed rules about what to say or do in any situation because it depends on what is appropriate and helpful for the others. The best thing is to be a good friend at any time in any situation.

We can encourage any interest in the understanding of life now. Gradually there may be more interest in discussing the truth and the cause of all difficulties. Without understanding, there cannot be a remedy for wrong thinking and all kinds of disturbances in life. We can point out that nothing is permanent, life changes all the time.

The help has to be according to the others' interest and what is useful to them. It may be that we can only offer practical help with daily living for now. We help the best we can with kindness and without expectations.

> Bhikkhus, possessing five factors, speech is well spoken, not badly spoken; it is blameless and beyond reproach by the wise. What five? It is spoken at the proper time; what is said is true; it is spoken gently; what is said is beneficial; it is spoken with a mind of loving-kindness. Possessing these five factors, speech is well spoken, not badly spoken; it is blameless and beyond reproach by the wise
>
> Aṅguttara Nikāya 5:198, Speech (Translated by Bhikkhu Bodhi)

65

Path to Enlightenment

The four iddhi-pādas are the bases (pāda) for spiritual power (iddhi) leading to enlightenment. These are chanda (interest), citta (consciousness), viriya (effort or patience) and vimaṃsā (understanding). Without interest in the truth, wholesome cittas, right effort and the development of right understanding, there cannot be any path to enlightenment.

If there is not the development of satipaṭṭhāna, direct understanding with awareness, there cannot be the development of the iddhi pādas. The development of samatha (calm) leading to jhānas without the development of the understanding of the Truths is the wrong path (micchā paṭipadā).

> *Bhikkhus, those who have neglected the four bases for spiritual power have neglected the noble path leading to the complete destruction of suffering. Those who have undertaken the four bases for spiritual power have undertaken the noble path leading to the complete destruction of suffering.*
>
> Saṃyutta Nikāya 2:2, Neglected (Translated by Bhikkhu Bodhi)

66

Vegetarian

Ngu Hoa brought up the topic of being vegetarian. She wondered whether it helps to reduce killing. Surely there is more mettā (loving kindness) in this way?

Mettā does not depend on being vegetarian or non-vegetarian. Being vegetarian does not reduce killing. Even if we do not buy meat, there will be killing anyway. Instead of just wanting to be vegetarian to reduce killing, it is better to understand why it is not good to kill. Otherwise there is no understanding of the real cause of killing.

> *Ajahn Sujin:* Can you tell people not to get angry? It doesn't have anything to do with being vegetarian at all. What about not eating meat but still having lobha (attachment), dosa (aversion) and moha (ignorance) as before? Does it help?
>
> *Ngu Hoa:* No
>
> *AS:* So the best thing is to understand the truth of what appears now, otherwise there must be killing from life to life. Didn't the Buddha eat meat?

When one does not want to eat meat, there may be clinging to the self. The truth is that there is no person, just realities arising and falling by different conditions. It is better to know this than just clinging to being this or that kind of person. What you eat is not a fish or a cow but just a rūpa like other rūpas.

Someone asked about the danger of killing.

AS: What is killing?

Answer: dosa

AS: What is dosa? Is it you?

Dosa (aversion) is a mental factor which arises and falls away with unpleasant feeling. It does not belong to anyone.

When there is interest in the Teachings with the idea of a self it is not useful. There is still the idea that such realities belong to me or to someone else. All problems and whatever occurs in life can be known as only dhammas. This knowledge is quite a relief.

As long as there is no understanding of realities now it is just like living in a dream. The moment of understanding is like waking up from the dream. The intellectual understanding is like the map that reveals what is hidden.

> **Those who are rough, violent, backbiters,
> betrayers of friends, cruel-hearted, arrogant,
> miserly, who do not give to anyone:
> this is carrion, but not the eating of meat.**
>
> Suttanipāta 2:2, Carrion (Translated by Bhikkhu Bodhi)

67

Suicide of Monks

Vincent raised a question about the occasion when the Buddha taught about the impurity of the body to the bhikkhus at Vesāli, which appeared to result in many of them committing suicide.

Only the Buddha knew all the underlying tendencies and dispositions of those he addressed and what was most useful for them to hear.

Without understanding the realities in life there cannot be any appreciation of the Buddha's wisdom and understanding of dhammas as conditioned and anattā.

It is more important to understand what the truth is now than to just talk about the past or the future.

> *Ajahn Sujin*: Understand that what is now is life. It's endless when we just think about this and that question about why such and such happened. Without understanding this moment, can you understand who the Buddha is and what he taught?

> *Why did he speak thus? In the past, it is said, five hundred men earned their living together as hunters. They were reborn in hell, but later, through some good kamma, they took rebirth as human beings and went forth as monks under the Blessed One. However, a portion of their original bad kamma had gained the opportunity to ripen during this fortnight and was due to bring on their deaths both by suicide and homicide.*
>
> *The Blessed One foresaw this and realized he could do nothing about it. Among those monks, some were worldlings, some stream-enterers, some once-returners, some nonreturners, some arahants. The arahants would not take rebirth, the other noble disciples were bound for a happy rebirth, but the worldlings were of uncertain destiny.*
>
> *The Buddha spoke of the foulness to remove their attachment to the body so that they would lose their fear of death and could thus be reborn in heaven. Therefore he spoke on foulness in order to help them, not with the intention of extolling death. Realizing he could not turn back the course of events, he went into seclusion to avoid being present when destiny took its toll.*

Commentary to Saṃyutta Nikāya 54:9 At Vesāli (Translated by Bhikkhu Bodhi)

68

What is Practice?

Ajahn Sujin spoke at length in a Chinese discussion about the dhammas (realities) which make up life now. A friend asked whether this was related to practice.

> *Ajahn Sujin:* What is practice?
>
> *Friend:* There are many different methods to cultivate sati (awareness). Which one is correct?
>
> *AS:* What is the purpose of practice and what does it mean?
>
> *F:* To calm the mind.
>
> *AS:* Do you know what the mind is? Can you calm hearing now?
>
> *F:* No.
>
> *AS:* So what is the truth of mind now?
>
> *F:* There is thinking, there is mind.
>
> *AS:* Can you calm that which has arisen and fallen away already?

In other words, whatever dhamma arises, falls away instantly.

When there is the idea of practising to calm the mind, there is the wrong idea that the mind or the present reality lasts and can be the object of such calming. There is also the idea that we can practise or we can do such calming.

This is not the understanding of what has been conditioned already that is not in the control of any self.

For there is suffering, but none who suffers:
Doing exists although there is no doer;
Extinction is but no extinguished person;
Although there is a path, there is no goer.

Visuddhimagga XVI, 90 (Translated by Bhikkhu Ñāṇamoli)

69

Accumulations

Every dhamma passes like a flash. It is gone immediately, but straight away there is the idea of someone or some thing. Life is just a moment of experiencing. Without any experiencing, there is no life.

There was a discussion about the disadvantage of unwholesome mental states and the advantage of wholesome states. There has to be the understanding that none of them belong to a self.

When there is anger what is it angry at? The other person cannot harm you, only one's own defilements can harm, especially the ignorance and wrong understanding about people and a self. We are always thinking about this or that story about people and situations, but nothing can arise now without conditions. Each has their own accumulations to think and behave in different ways.

Aṅgulimāla was a ruthless murderer who became fully enlightened when he heard the Buddha's words. It shows how unexpected and unpredictable the various accumulations are. No one imagined all the murderer's strong unwholesome tendencies would be completely eradicated through great insight into the Noble Truths.

> *Bhikkhus, there are these three kinds of persons found existing in the world. What three? One whose mind is like an open sore, one whose mind is like lightning, and one whose mind is like a diamond.*
>
> *(1) And what, bhikkhus, is the person whose mind is like an open sore? Here, some person is prone to anger and easily exasperated. Even if he is criticized slightly*

he loses his temper and becomes irritated, hostile, and stubborn; he displays irritation, hatred, and bitterness. Just as a festering sore, if struck by a stick or a shard, will discharge even more matter, so too some person here is prone to anger and displays irritation, hatred, and bitterness. This person is said to have a mind like an open sore.

(2) And what is the person whose mind is like lightning? Here, some person understands as it really is: 'This is suffering,' and 'This is the origin of suffering,' and 'This is the cessation of suffering,' and 'This is the way leading to the cessation of suffering.' Just as, in the dense darkness of night, a man with good sight can see forms by a flash of lightning, so too some person here understands as it really is: 'This is suffering,' and 'This is the origin of suffering,' and 'This is the cessation of suffering,' and 'This is the way leading to the cessation of suffering.' This person is said to have a mind like lightning.

(3) And what is the person whose mind is like a diamond? Here, with the destruction of the taints, some person realizes for himself with direct knowledge, in this very life, the taintless liberation of mind, liberation by wisdom, and having entered upon it, dwells in it. Just as there is nothing that a diamond cannot cut, whether gem or stone, so too, with the destruction of the taints, some person realizes for himself with direct knowledge, in this very life, the taintless liberation of mind, liberation by wisdom, and and having entered upon it, dwells in it. This person is said to have a mind like a diamond.

These, bhikkhus, are the three kinds of persons found existing in the world.

Aṅguttara Nikāya 3:25, Diamond (Translated by Bhikkhu Bodhi)

70

Appears Well

Nina asked about the Pāli term for "appears well" when it is said that, when there is direct understanding of the reality appearing, the object appears well. I mentioned that the Pāli word suvidita is used in the texts. However, we were reminded not to cling to any word.

Now, does the object appear well? The understanding always comes back to this moment, otherwise we are just lost in stories about terms, definitions and details about realities, without any understanding appearing now, such as the seeing or thinking.

Ya Ya asked about the meaning of the Yamaka Sutta. Yamaka had expounded a wrong view with regard to arahants, the view that these are beings who are annihilated at death.

Ajahn Sujin: Who is seeing now?

There must be understanding of what appears otherwise whatever we hear or read will be misunderstood, such as when there is the idea that "I am seeing" or what is seen is another person. At such moments there is no understanding of what is the wrong understanding.

Venerable Sāriputta explained to Yamaka the truth about the various dhammas in life as anattā. All conditioned dhammas arise and cease. For the arahant, the arising and ceasing of dhammas comes to an end at death. Yamaka understood this well.

> *If, friend Yamaka, they were to ask you: 'Friend Yamaka, when a bhikkhu is an arahant, one whose taints are destroyed, what happens to him with the breakup of the body, after death?'—being asked thus, what would you answer?*
>
> *If they were to ask me this, friend, I would answer thus: 'Friends, form is impermanent; what is impermanent is suffering; what is suffering has ceased and passed away. Feeling is impermanent; what is impermanent is suffering; what is suffering has ceased and passed*

away. Perception is impermanent; what is impermanent is suffering; what is suffering has ceased and passed away. Volitional formations are impermanent; what is impermanent is suffering; what is suffering has ceased and passed away. Consciousness is impermanent; what is impermanent is suffering; what is suffering has ceased and passed away.' Being asked thus, friend, I would answer in such a way.

Saṃyutta Nikāya 22:85, Yamaka (Translated by Bhikkhu Bodhi)

2
June 2021

71

The Seed and Fertiliser for the Path

Azita asked about the three kinds of understanding (paññā) that are: suta-maya-paññā (understanding based on hearing), cintā-maya-paññā (understanding based on wise considering) and bhāvanā-maya-paññā (understanding based on the development).

These terms refer to the development of understanding of the Path. Suta-maya-paññā is the hearing about dhammas and appreciating the benefit of understanding them. It brings about firmer understanding about what life is now. It is not just hearing or reading the Buddha's words again and again without understanding. That cannot be suta-maya-paññā. The seed has to be planted to understand realities as not self. When there is more and more suta maya paññā, there is more and more confidence in the truth.

Cintā-maya-paññā is the wise thinking and considering about what is true. It is the fertiliser for understanding to grow. Usually there is thinking about other things throughout the day, but when there is enough intellectual understanding it can condition wise considering about what has been heard. Gradually there may be less thinking about other ideas and topics and more wise consideration about what is true and beneficial now.

Bhāvanā-maya-paññā is the development of direct understanding of dhammas to realise the truth. Without suta-maya-paññā and cinta-maya-paññā having developed, there cannot be bhāvanā-māya-paññā. It has to be right understanding of what appears now. There has to be a lot of hearing and considering about the various realities which make up life for there to be bhāvanā-māya-paññā which understands them well and clearly.

We also read in the Paṭisambhidāmagga about another three kinds of understanding (ñāṇa): suta-maya-ñāṇa, sīla-maya-ñāṇa and samādhi-bhāvanā-maya-ñāṇa.

Suta-maya-ñāna refers to paññā gained by listening attentively to the Buddha's Teachings as before.

Sīla-maya-ñāṇa refers to paññā gained by restraint from misconduct and understanding of the danger of such ill deeds through understanding of dhammas as anattā.

Samādhi-bhāvanā-maya-ñāṇa is the concentration of mind which occurs after restraint from misconduct. It develops with the firm and clear understanding of realities as not self.

When there is no understanding, it is easy to read any of the texts with the wrong idea of a self doing or practising something. This is why what is most precious in life is the right understanding, the right view of the path, which leads to the development of all kinds of wholesome qualities. Without the seed and fertiliser, right understanding is impossible.

> **Bhikkhus, I do not see even a single thing on account of which unarisen wholesome qualities arise and arisen wholesome qualities increase and expand so much**

as right view. For one of right view, unarisen wholesome qualities arise and arisen wholesome qualities increase and expand.

Aṅguttara Nikāya 1:307, Second sub-chapter (Translated by Bhikkhu Bodhi)

72

Letting Go

In a Chinese discussion, Kwun Yuan asked about "letting go". He practices breath exercises and mentioned "being in the emptiness".

> *Ajahn Sujin:* Would you like to understand or would you like to "let go"?
>
> *KY*: To let go of the result.
>
> *AS*: Is that understanding or just wanting to let go?
>
> *KY*: If there's understanding, there's letting go.
>
> *AS*: Understanding of what? This is the point.
>
> *KY:* For example, understanding the breath.
>
> *AS*: What is the reality of breath?
>
> (no answer)
>
> *AS*: So how can there be letting go if there's no understanding of what is to be let go of? In order to understand "letting go", there must be the understanding of the object of letting go. There must be understanding of the truth, otherwise it's just thinking about it. When we say "breath", is there any truth of it? It needs reflecting on, considering, until there is understanding of the truth of it. Is there breath now? If we don't call it breath, is it still there?
>
> *KY:* Yes.

AS: What is the characteristic of that? It's a reality, so what's the characteristic we call breath?

KY: It's felt through the body-sense.

AS: So this is the way of "letting go" of the idea of "I am breathing". Breath is conditioned by citta. It's just what can be touched. It's the hardness there, not the other hardness. It doesn't belong to anyone and it's just conditioned by citta. Otherwise, without any understanding, there is just the idea of "I am breathing". There must be the understanding of breath as it is, otherwise there cannot be letting go of the idea "I can breathe" or the letting go of ignorance and the wrong view of self.

In the end there must be the letting go of all wrong view of whatever is conditioned. Each word of understanding will help let go of ignorance and wrong view very gradually.

When there is right understanding there cannot be the following of any practice. There is the understanding that there is no one to do anything. There has to be more and more letting go of wrong understanding for the reality experienced to be clearly known.

> *Bhikkhus, for a person of wrong view, whatever bodily kamma, verbal kamma, and mental kamma he instigates and undertakes in accordance with that view, and whatever his volition, yearning, inclination, and volitional activities, all lead to what is unwished for, undesired, and disagreeable, to harm and suffering. For what reason? Because the view is bad.*
>
> *Suppose, bhikkhus, a seed of neem, bitter cucumber, or bitter gourd were planted in moist soil. Whatever nutrients it takes up from the soil and from the water would all lead to its bitter, pungent, and disagreeable flavor. For what reason? Because the seed is bad. So too, for a person of wrong view, whatever bodily kamma, verbal kamma, and mental kamma he instigates and undertakes in accordance with that view, and whatever his*

volition, yearning, inclination, and volitional activities, all lead to what is unwished for, undesired, and disagreeable, to harm and suffering. For what reason? Because the view is bad.

Aṅguttara Nikāya 1:314, Second sub-chapter (Translated by Bhikkhu Bodhi)

73

Breath

Lily asked us more about breath and breathing.

The point of listening to the Teachings is to understand dhammas as anattā, not self. Whether we call it breath or hardness or softness, there is the reality which can be the object of understanding. Usually the reality is taken for something again and again.

If there is no understanding of what appears now we just continue to talk about other things as usual, including stories we have heard or read about the Buddha's Teachings, such as those about breath. What appears now?

We have often heard or read about nāmas (the realities which can experience an object) and rūpas (the realities which cannot experience anything). What is nāma now? What is rūpa now? All dhammas that arise are conditioned and fall away instantly, they are not in anyone's control. So it is impossible to concentrate on any particular reality, such as breath, to make it appear. By the time there is concentrating on a particular object, the reality has long since fallen away, but one is bound by desire for it.

The thinking, with the idea of a self, tries to understand all the details beyond one's ability to comprehend them. So many details can only be understood by the Buddha's accumulations or those of his great disciples. For example, does breath appear now? Is it there to be known or not yet?

Hardness (or softness) is there and appearing, but we don't have to call it breath or anything else. If one tries to understand breath, it is impossible for understanding and awareness to arise. What is touched now? Is it breath? Everyone understands that there is breath near the nostrils but when the tangible object is experienced it is not what we are used to calling breath. Desire for results is so subtle now.

Only realities, i.e. cittas, cetasikas and rūpas, can appear. Only direct understanding of the reality appearing at present can eliminate doubt. The point of the Teachings is not to learn more words or to cling with desire to particular experiences, but to understand the truth now.

> *By what is the world bound?*
> *By the removal of what is it freed?*
> *What is it that one must forsake*
> *To cut off all bondage?*
>
> *By desire is the world bound;*
> *By the removal of desire it is freed.*
> *Desire is what one must forsake*
> *To cut off all bondage.*
>
> Saṃyutta Nikāya 1:69, Desire (Translated by Bhikkhu Bodhi)

74

Unknown Defilements

The anusayas (latent unwholesome tendencies) are very subtle. They never appear because they never arise. However, if there were no anusayas there could not be any akusala qualities arising as these all depend on the anusayas. The anusayas are carried forward with each citta. They are:

   attachment to sense objects (kāmarāga)
   aversion (paṭigha)

wrong view (diṭṭhi)
doubt (vicikicchā)
conceit (māna)
clinging to existence (bhavarāga)
ignorance (avijjā)

The anusayas are like germs that cannot be known directly but are ready to "taint" the cittas, to condition akusala cittas to arise. Each citta itself is pure (paṇḍara) but it is tainted because of the anusayas which have not been eradicated.

Without the development of right understanding, the anusayas can never be eradicated. There has to be the gradual elimination of these tendencies before they can be eradicated stage by stage.

The anusayas of wrong view and doubt are eradicated at the first stage of enlightenment. The anusayas of attachment to sense objects and aversion are eradicated at the third stage and the anusayas of conceit, clinging to existence and ignorance are eradicated at the fourth stage, when no more defilements can arise again.

Without anusayas there cannot be āsavas (intoxicants) which do arise. These are very subtle kinds of clinging to sense objects and existence, wrong view and ignorance which arise instantly after seeing, hearing, smelling, tasting and touching.

Whenever there is the very subtle and unknown idea of something or someone as existing, there are the āsavas of ignorance and wrong view. Any moments of understanding are very brief and cannot be compared to the countless moments when the āsavas are arising, much more than imagined.

A friend mentioned there is a lot of dreaming and thinking. What about the āsavas arising long before there is the idea of a particular story or person or thing or situation? Without the anusayas, no akusala thinking at all could arise.

It is customary to call long-fermented madira wines, etc., intoxicants. If by long fermentation they are named intoxicants, then these mental states are also worthy of

> *the name. For it has been said: 'No ultimate point of ignorance is apparent so that one may say, once there was no ignorance'.*
>
> Atthasālinī (The Expositor) I, Part I, Ch II (Translated by Pe Maung Tin)

75

Khandha and Upādāna khandha

Each conditioned reality is a khandha. Khandha refers to the reality which arises and falls away. Any rūpa is rūpa khandha, any vedanā (feeling) is vedanā khandha, any saññā (memory) is saññā khandha, any other cetasika (mental factor) is saṅkhāra khandha and any kind of citta is viññāna khandha.

There can be clinging (upādāna), to any of these khandhas. For example, when a rūpa arises, it can be the object of clinging before it falls away. Only when it arises is it rūpa khandha and only when there is clinging is it upādāna khandha.

Upādāna clings to different rūpas very much, such as when wishing to see what is visible, wishing to experience a rūpa such as softness again and again or enjoying the taste of food. When it is pleasant, there is pleasant feeling which is also the object of clinging throughout the day and which leads to the searching for more pleasant feeling again and again. There is just the wanting of that which is remembered by saññā. There is clinging to the various memories, different mental factors and moments of seeing, hearing and other kinds of experiences as well.

Even the rūpas of the Buddha's body are upādāna khandha when they are the object of clinging by others. Any reality except the lokuttara (supramundane) dhammas can be objects of clinging (upādāniya).

That which is only hardness is taken for other people or things, but it is just hardness. It is not wise to cling to hardness again and again. What is seen are just different colours. What is the use of clinging to light or colour? The pleasant feelings which are the object of clinging have all gone when there is dreaming about them. When there is wise reflection and understanding, there is calmness and peace from clinging and disturbance at such moments.

Between birth and death there is nothing remaining. Whatever arose has gone, never to return again. To live alone means to live with understanding that there is no one at all. The true teacher and good friend is one who does not encourage attachment to the khandhas. This means there is no encouragement to cling again and again to what is experienced through the sense doors, to pleasant feelings and memories or to any kind of experience at all.

> *And what, bhikkhus, are the five aggregates subject to clinging?*
>
> *Whatever kind of form there is, whether past, future, or present, internal or external, gross or subtle, inferior or superior, far or near, that is tainted (sāsava), that can be clung to (upādāniya): this is called the form aggregate subject to clinging (upādānakkhandha).*
>
> *Whatever kind of feeling there is ... that is tainted, that can be clung to: this is called the feeling aggregate subject to clinging.*
>
> *Whatever kind of perception there is... that is tainted, that can be clung to: this is called the perception aggregate subject to clinging.*
>
> *Whatever kind of volitional formations there are... that are tainted, that can be clung to: these are called the volitional formations aggregate subject to clinging.*
>
> *Whatever kind of consciousness there is, whether past, future, or present, internal or external, gross or subtle, inferior or superior, far or near, that is tainted, that can be clung to: this is called the consciousness aggregate subject to clinging.*
>
> *These, bhikkhus, are called the five aggregates subject to clinging.*
>
> Saṃyutta Nikāya 22:48, Aggregates (Translated by Bhikkhu Bodhi)

76

Nothing, Something, Nothing

Each moment of consciousness arises and falls away instantly, one at a time without any gap. After the previous citta has fallen away, the next citta arises immediately. There cannot be more than one citta at any time; seeing and hearing cannot be present at the same time.

Each reality arises and disappears very rapidly. There must be bhavaṅga cittas (life-continuum consciousness) before the eye-door cittas arise. There are many, many moments of bhavaṅga cittas when nothing appears through the sense doors or mind door.

Understanding of dhammas (realities) as anattā (not self) begins with much wise considering about the truth. Gradually the conditioned nature of the reality may appear well. There can be conditions for the understanding that the reality now arising did not exist the moment before its arising and will cease to exist the moment it has fallen away. This truth can be summarised as "nothing, then something, then nothing".

Life exists in a very short moment. That which has gone is nothing, but usually what has gone is taken for things and people. When there is vipassanā (insight) understanding, the paññā experiences the object clearer and clearer. However, there has to be firm intellectual understanding to condition any direct understanding of the truth.

When paññā is strong enough, there is no trouble or disturbance about any dhamma arising unexpectedly because it is understood as anattā, not in anyone's control. Paññā does not mind whether it is kindness or attachment, calm or anger experienced. It just understands whatever appears.

Without the development of right understanding, there is always the study with the idea of self and the clinging to self grows and grows.

The only way is to understand what appears clearer and clearer, little by little, like when holding the knife or adze handle which is very slowly, imperceptibly, worn away.

> *When, bhikkhus, a carpenter or a carpenter's apprentice looks at the handle of his adze, he sees the impressions of his fingers and his thumb, but he does not know: 'So much of the adze handle has been worn away today, so much yesterday, so much earlier.' But when it has worn away, the knowledge occurs to him that it has worn away.*
>
> *So too, bhikkhus, when a bhikkhu dwells devoted to development, even though no such knowledge occurs to him: 'So much of my taints has been worn away today, so much yesterday, so much earlier,' yet when they are worn away, the knowledge occurs to him that they have been worn away.*
>
> Saṃyutta Nikāya 22:101, The Adze Handle (Translated by Bhikkhu Bodhi)

77

The Point of Understanding

There was a question in the Chinese discussion about why lobha (attachment) and moha (ignorance) are unwholesome roots.

Saṃsāra (the cycle of birth and death) continues because ignorance and attachment have not been eradicated. There should be the knowing of the present dhammas in order to know the roots. The fruit and the leaves may appear, but do the roots? Even though there is attachment now, is it known? Ignorance is not known now either.

There is lobha almost all the time. There is always wanting something. There is attachment to what is seen immediately and it is unknown. If there is still the idea of "something existing", it is the object of attachment with wrong view.

Whatever arises is just a moment in a lifetime, a moment in saṃsāra. The point of understanding is not to find the meaning of words but to understand what appears now as a reality, which is anattā. Usually the idea of self does not show up but it is arising again and again as an āsava (the very subtle defilement). What appears now? It cannot be known by just thinking about the meaning.

Studying the subtlety of all dhammas is the only way to eradicate attachment, such as the wanting to understand and the desire to eliminate defilements quickly.

Lily asked whether there was a need to observe what is present. There is no one who develops the path, no one who can observe or do anything. Only listening and considering carefully from hearing the Teachings without the idea of "I" at all will lead to understanding. Without hearing the words of the Buddha, it is impossible to understand realities now. These are just the different nāmas and rūpas arising and falling away, the realities which experience and those which cannot experience anything.

To go somewhere or to do something with the idea of "I can do" or "I can practice" is wrong. It indicates no understanding of the truth of this moment and just leads to the wrong path. The point of understanding is to develop the right path which leads to the eradication of all defilements.

> *What others speak of as happiness,*
> *that the noble ones speak of as suffering.*
>
> *What others speak of as suffering,*
> *that the noble ones have known as happiness.*
>
> *Behold this Dhamma hard to comprehend:*
> *here the foolish are bewildered.*
>
> Suttanipāta 3:12, 762, Happiness and Suffering (Translated by Bhikkhu Bodhi)

78

A Moment

There was a question about birth, death and personality.

For this life, the paṭisandhi citta (birth consciousness), the cuti citta (death consciousness) and all the bhavaṅga (life continuum) cittas are conditioned by the same kamma from a past life. As long as the bhavaṅga cittas keep arising in this life there will be this particular personality. It is impossible to know in which past life the kamma arose that conditioned the birth and the subsequent bhavaṅga cittas in this life. The different life-spans depend on the kamma which produced the paṭisandhi citta, all the bhavaṅga cittas and the cuti citta.

Life is just a current of bhavaṅga cittas interrupted by sense and mind door processes. No matter what the plane of existence, the first process of cittas arises in the mind-door with lobha (atttachment). It is like when waking up from sleep and clinging instantly to something pleasant which is not a sense object.

The arising and falling away of each citta is a momentary death (khaṇika maraṇa). This is death in the absolute sense. Everyone is going to die at the end of this life. This is the sammuti maraṇa (conventional death). The third kind of death is samuccheda maraṇa at the death of the arahat, the final "cutting off" of all life.

We cannot know whether seeing or hearing now is the result of the same kamma which produced the paṭisandhi citta in this life. If it is an unpleasant sense object it cannot be the result of the same kamma because the paṭisandhi citta for a human existence must be the result of kusala kamma. Whether it's the life of a human or a cat or a dog or an insect, there are pleasant and unpleasant sense objects experienced.

It cannot be known what past kusala or akusala kamma will bring what result. Painful bodily feelings are the result of akusala kamma but it cannot be known which kamma in which lifetime produced such results. Whatever arises just lasts for a moment and is gone. Understanding is a condition for more wholesome mental states and deeds. The results we experience, such as the painful bodily feeling, are not caused by the others' deeds.

The best thing in life is understanding any reality as it truly is.

No matter what the topic taught by the Buddha, whether it be birth, death, bhavaṅga cittas, sense experiences, personality, kamma, the khandhas or anything else, it is just about different realities arising and falling away. There is never any atta, any self, or thing to be found.

> *Since states (dhammas) last but a moment's time*
> *Those aggregates (khandhas), by which was done*
> *The odious act, have ceased, so now*
> *What is it you are angry with?*
>
> Visuddhimagga IX, 22 (Translated by Bhikkhu Ñāṇamoli)

79

Protection

There was a question about "ārakkhā gocara" in a Vietnamese discussion.

Ārakkhā means protection. Gocara refers to the object of understanding. When there is right understanding about the truth of the reality appearing, there is guarding or protection from unwholesome states. Ārakkhā gocara refers to the understanding that protects from experiencing the wrong object with wrong understanding.

Without the development of understanding through careful consideration it is impossible to get used to experiencing the presently appearing object with awareness and understanding. This is understanding which conditions the ārakkhā gocara, the protection from akusala states. There is no self, no one who can make understanding develop to be a protection or who can hasten such development.

Firmer and firmer understanding of realities develops and there is more and more confidence that no person or thing can be found. Now there are just different moments of seeing, hearing, smelling, tasting, touching and thinking arising and falling away very quickly. The understanding develops until it is the direct understanding of the truth. It is the "binding" or "anchoring" of the understanding to what appears, never moving away from this moment, like the anchor of a ship that does not move away.

Understanding develops so slowly because of the great amount of ignorance, attachment and other defilements. The proof of what the Buddha taught is always the understanding now.

At a moment of direct understanding of reality there is no thought about its development or protection, but the understanding has been accumulated to condition such direct understanding of the truth of what appears now.

> *Move in your own resort [gocara], bhikkhus, in your own ancestral domain. Māra will not gain access to those who move in their own resort, in their own ancestral domain; Māra will not get a hold on them.*
> *And what is a bhikkhu's resort, his own ancestral domain? It is the four establishments of mindfulness.*
> Saṃyutta Nikāya 47:6, The Hawk (Translated by Bhikkhu Bodhi)

80

A Certain Person

Nina raised some points about understanding realities as not self. It seems there are friends in different places.

Ajahn Sujin asked her where she is now. Where is Sarah? Where is Lodewijk? There is only seeing, hearing and thinking now.

It seems there is a self seeing or thinking but we should not underestimate any of the words of the Buddha such as those about self-view or ignorance when there's the idea of "I'm sitting now".

> *Ajahn Sujin:* Can hardness sit? Can the ear-sense sit? Where is the self, "I"? If there is nothing at all, can there be the world? Whatever arises is a reality which is taken for being some thing.

Nina: How does Ajahn know the reality has gone and never comes back?

AS: Paññā understands and develops. No other way! Are you Nina van Gorkom?

N: Yes!

AS: See - someone! I am "I" only in this life. What you like and are satisfied with is not there anymore. Should you be proud of it? There are the arising and falling away of realities all the time. All completely gone. It brings the understanding of nimitta (signs of realities).

There was a further question about accumulating understanding. Nothing can be remembered from past lives. If there is conceit about the accumulations to be a certain person in this life it is so unhelpful because it just leads to more and more pride about being a certain person in future too.

> **Just as people throw clean things and dirty things, excrement, urine, spittle, pus, and blood on the earth, and the earth is not repelled, humiliated, and disgusted because of that, so too, Rāhula, develop meditation (bhāvanā) that is like the earth; for when you develop meditation that is like the earth, arisen agreeable and disagreeable contacts will not invade your mind and remain.**
>
> Majjhima Nikāya 62, Mahārāhulovāda Sutta (Translated by Bhikkhu Ñāṇamoli and Bhikkhu Bodhi)

81

The Simple Life

Tadao said that he found a simple lifestyle to be preferable to develop more understanding of the Dhamma.

Achan Sujin stressed that when we think a simple lifestyle is better for the development of understanding it indicates no understanding of the truth about realities in daily life. There has to be the letting go of whatever thinking there is about different situations as being preferable.

For example, which is preferable out of a luxurious lifestyle like King Bimbisāra led with understanding or a simple lifestyle with lots of clinging and no understanding? As paññā develops it lets go of such ideas and clinging. It understands that whatever life is at this moment must be by conditions, not by anyone's will. There is not enough understanding when there is the idea of "I would prefer a simple life" or "a simple life would be better".

To respect the Buddha means to respect the truth according to his words. He taught everyone to understand, not just to follow. Only the understanding of what is true and what appears now can let go of wrong understanding. In truth there is no one, no "me", just realities which arise and fall away instantly. Seeing consciousness sees a visible object, not a rich or poor person, a beautiful or ugly scene.

Without understanding it's meaningless to say one respects or takes refuge in the Buddha. There must be respect for the truth, to begin to respect the great virtues and wisdom of the Buddha.

Indeed, "Buddha" means great understanding or truth.

> *But, bhikkhus, when a Tathāgata arises in the world, an Arahant, a Perfectly Enlightened One, then there is the manifestation of great light and radiance; then no blinding darkness prevails, no dense mass of darkness; then there is the explaining, teaching, proclaiming, establishing, disclosing, analysing, and elucidating of the Four Noble Truths. What four? The noble truth of suffering, the noble truth of the origin of suffering, the noble truth of the cessation of suffering, the noble truth of the way leading to the cessation of suffering.*
>
> Saṃyutta Nikāya 56:38, The Sun (Translated by Bhikkhu Bodhi)

82

Trapped by the Idea of Self

The idea of a self hinders all the time. For example when we ask "Can I know this?" or "Is this right?" or "How can I understand?", the idea of a self is preventing the natural understanding of what appears now. It is not a matter of trying to do something or trying to understand.

The Teachings of the Buddha reveal the subtlety of dhammas, the subtlety of the truth of life now and the trap of attachment. Without the Buddha's enlightenment it would be impossible to know. There has to be the direct awareness and understanding of what one has learned.

Even visible object which is seen now is not known. There are ideas of many things around and it is very difficult to go to the truth which is hidden by ignorance. There is nothing in what is seen, but it appears as a thing such as a table, a computer, an arm or a leg.

Attachment is lurking all the time, clinging to an idea of a self. It has to be eradicated but it is so very deeply rooted and prolific.

When understanding develops, it is not hindered by the idea of "I want to know this" or "What is this?". All dhammas are anattā (not self). Without this understanding the idea of "I" is always ready to arise. There has to be the gradual letting go of the wrong idea of self from the very beginning. Even doubt now can be understood as not self.

No matter how weak, the careful consideration with understanding has to develop to know what appears so that there can be the direct understanding of one reality at a time. The reality which has just fallen away is nothing but it is taken to be something, so it's atta saññā (wrong memory of self) again and again until the lurking wrong view of self is eradicated.

> *Such is form, such its origin, such its passing away;*
> *such is feeling, such its origin, such its passing away; such*

> *is perception, such its origin, such its passing away; such are volitional formations, such their origin, such their passing away; such is consciousness, such its origin, such its passing away.*
>
> *Thus when this exists, that comes to be; with the arising of this, that arises. When this does not exist, that does not come to be; with the cessation of this, that ceases.*

Saṃyutta Nikāya 12:21, The Ten Powers (Translated by Bhikkhu Bodhi)

83

Conceit

We shared examples of common māna (conceit). I gave examples of observing the clothes or hair-styles or backgrounds of others during a zoom discussion. There are subtle comparisons so often during the day. Ajahn Sujin also gave one example by asking Ann "Are you Ann Marshall?"

Surely there is the idea of one's importance instantly, like "waving the banner"? There can be pride in almost anything for a very brief moment.

When we think of our hand and how it is different from another's hand, it may be with māna or with diṭṭhi (wrong view) but it cannot be with both at the same time, even though attachment must arise with both of them.

The anusaya (unwholesome latent tendency) of conceit is only eradicated at the moment of becoming an arahat.

> *Humility is meekness and humble behavior, possessing which a person is without conceit, without vanity, like a foot-wiping cloth, like a bull with cut-off horns, like a defanged viper—docile, tender, soft-spoken. This is humility.*

> It is called a blessing because it is a cause for obtaining such excellent qualities as fame. As he said, 'One of humble behavior, not stiff with pride, gains fame,' and so forth (DN III 192).

Commentary to Suttanipāta 4, The Minor Chapter 265, Blessings (Translated by Bhikkhu Bodhi)

84

The Signs & Details of Realities

Vi Van asked a question about concepts and realities in a Vietnamese discussion.

The world is experienced in terms of concepts, but without realities there would be no concepts of people and different things like tables and chairs.

Because of the rapidity of the arising and falling away of cittas experiencing their objects through sense and mind doors, there is the idea of a whole, an image of someone or of a table, chair or finger. Just as it takes not one dot but many dots to make a picture, so it takes many experiences through the sense and mind doors before there is an image of a mountain or a lake. It seems as if they are seen at once, but there are countless moments of seeing and thinking.

As it says in the Satipaṭṭhāna Sutta, if the butcher does not skin and cut up the cow into different parts it is still seen as a cow. When it is cut up it is no longer taken for a cow. What is seen now is just visible object or colour.

There are so many elements arising and falling away now so that which is seen is not that which we are used to taking for being seen. We think we see a table but what is seen is not a table, it's just the visible object. Because of ignorance, the truth about realities is covered up. Only right understanding can reveal the truth.

Without the Buddha's Teachings it would be impossible to know that which is hidden. We live in a dream world from birth until death if there is no understanding of the realities.

Tinh-Y asked about the nimitta and anubyañjana, the signs and details of realities. Two apples or cars or twins may look the same but when we look carefully they are different. This is because the details of what is seen are not the same. Likewise there may be the same good smells of food, but they are never the same. They always have slight differences. The shape of the nose, the eyes, the eyebrows are different by their details, their anubyañjana. If we cannot tell the difference, it is because we do not mind or think about such details.

Each word of the Teachings represents realities which can be studied and understood, but it needs careful consideration. There has to be firmer and firmer understanding of realities as not self to understand that what arises now can never arise again in saṃsāra (the cycle of birth and death).

> *Again, bhikkhus, a bhikkhu reviews this same body, however it is placed, however disposed, by way of elements thus: 'In this body there are the earth element, the water element, the fire element, and the air element.' Just as though a skilled butcher or his apprentice had killed a cow and was seated at the crossroads with it cut up into pieces; so too, a bhikkhu reviews this same body... by way of elements thus: 'In this body there are the earth element, the water element, the fire element, and the air element.'*
>
> Majjhima Nikāya 10, The Foundations of Mindfulness (Translated by Bhikkhu Ñāṇamoli and Bhikkhu Bodhi)

3
July 2021

85

How to Cultivate the Way

Lily asked how to cultivate the way to directly experience dhammas. Ajahn Sujin stressed that this is not the way, however, because there is the idea of one's self trying to do something. If there is no understanding of dhammas the understanding goes the wrong way.

This is very important from the beginning because it is so easy to go wrong with the idea of a self. The path is just to understand the absolute truth that there is no one, no thing, no self at all.

Would you like to understand what appears now or would you like to look for another way or short-cut? Before beginning to understand the truth, nothing is understood at all. The different realities are covered up by ignorance very tightly. Only the words of the Buddha can open up the truth.

> *Suppose, friend, a man needing heartwood, seeking heartwood, wandering in search of heartwood, would take a sharp axe and enter a forest. There he would see the trunk of a large plantain tree, straight, fresh, without a fruit-bud core. He would cut it down at the root, cut off the crown, and unroll the coil. As he unrolls the coil, he would not find even softwood, let alone heartwood.*
>
> *So too, a bhikkhu does not recognize either a self or anything belonging to a self in these six bases for contact. Since he does not recognize anything thus, he does not cling to anything in the world. Not clinging, he is not agitated. Being unagitated, he personally attains Nibbāna. He understands: 'Destroyed is birth, the holy life has been lived, what had to be done has been done, there is no more for this state of being.'*

Saṃyutta Nikāya 35:234, Udāyi (Translated by Bhikkhu Bodhi)

86

Mettā to the Dead?

Tam Bach wondered why there cannot be mettā (loving kindness) towards the dead, because there can be the sharing of merit with those in other realms.

Ajahn Sujin suggested this was a long story about mettā. Is there mettā now? What is the point of thinking like this if there is no mettā now for those around us, on the street, or in the shops. It is just thinking about mettā instead of having mettā now. Is it possible to think about those who have died and no longer exist as we knew them, or can there be thinking kindly about those here and now?

There is attachment because there is not enough understanding of mettā, always thinking about the past ones and wishing to have mettā. The clinging is not known. It is taking for mettā what is not mettā. If there is mettā now, there can be mettā to ants, dogs, snakes or any beings around now. They can all be the dear ones.

It is not mettā to the one who has passed away because that person that person no longer exists. Why does one want to have mettā to that one? The one known as that person was just at that time.

Mettā is friendliness to be developed in daily life. It is friendliness to other beings with the understanding that no one is there. Everyone would like to have pleasant feeling and experience kindness, so when there is consideration with good-will for another, there is mettā.

> *Just as a mother would protect her son, her only son,*
>   *with her own life,*
> *so one should develop toward all beings*
> *a state of mind without boundaries.*
>
> *And toward the whole world*
> *one should develop loving-kindness,*
> *a state of mind without boundaries—*
> *above, below, and across—*
> *unconfined, without enmity, without adversaries."*
>
> Suttanipāta 1:8, Loving Kindness (Translated by Bhikkhu Bodhi)

87

The Truth is always the Truth

In a Chinese discussion, the different schools of Buddhism were mentioned. There was the suggestion that what is being taught by us is just one school.

> *Ajahn Sujin:* What is a "school"?
>
> *Answer:* A concept.
>
> *AS:* Yes, but what is it?
>
> *Answer:* A different view for explaining, even for understanding anattā. Different views, different perspectives to explain Dhamma from different ideas.

AS: Is now a "school"?

Answer: Now is not a "school".

AS: So where and what is a "school"?

Answer: It's an idea.

AS: So we learn about the Teachings of the Buddha with different ideas, but the Teachings are about everything which is now, never known before. There is seeing right now. Who knows what it is? There must be a reality which is different from that which is seen. Is this a "school"? Is it a "school" or the truth?

We never knew about such realities before listening to the Buddha. The truth is the truth no matter what different ideas we have. If anyone studies Theravāda without understanding, it's not Theravāda.

Each word of truth comes from the enlightenment of the Buddha. There is the experiencing now and that which is experienced, not under anyone's control at all.

It takes a long time to understand the truth, the words of the Buddha from his enlightenment and the way to experience the Four Noble Truths. This is the only way that there can be the understanding of the difference between avijjā (ignorance) and vijjā (wisdom).

> *Whether Tathāgatas arise in the world or not, it still remains a fact, a firm and necessary condition of existence, that all formations are impermanent, that all formations are suffering, that all things (dhammā) are non-self.*
>
> Aṅguttara Nikāya 3:136, Arising (Translated by Bhikkhu Bodhi)

88

Thira Saññā (Firm Remembrance)

In a Chinese discussion there was mention of thira saññā. This is the firm remembrance with confidence again and again of what is true. It is the proximate condition for sati (awareness). By listening, considering and reflecting over and over again, it is said "he recalls and recollects" (saritā anussaritā) the truth about realities. Such recollection conditions awareness with understanding at the presnt moment, instead of being lost in the world of ideas of people and things as usual. When direct awareness and understanding do not arise, the saññā is not thira, not firm. When what has been heard and considered is well remembered enough to condition direct awareness, thira saññā is there.

The following quote does not refer to book knowledge or memorisation as we know it, but to the understanding of realities appearing now. There may be recollecting a sutta we read years ago, or remembering a wise comment, which conditions sati (awareness) now. Sati and thira saññā arise together, conditioning each other.

> *He has learned much, remembers what he has learned, and consolidates what he has learned. Such teachings as are good in the beginning, good in the middle, and good in the end, with the right meaning and phrasing, and affirm a holy life that is utterly perfect and pure – such teachings as these he has learned much of, remembered, recited verbally, investigated with the mind and penetrated well by view.*
>
> Majjhima Nikāya 53, Sekha Sutta (Translated by Bhikkhu Ñāṇamoli and Bhikkhu Bodhi)

89

Pariyatti Understanding

Pariyatti is the right understanding of realities which is not yet direct understanding. There has to be patience to consider carefully what the realities are now as taught by the Buddha. There should not be any hurry at all because whether such understanding arises and develops depends on conditions. We miss the point when it is "I" again wanting to know this or that, "I" trying to speed up the Path.

If there is the idea that "I can try", "I will be aware" or "I will practice" there cannot be the right conditions for direct awareness. The sati (awareness) must be conditioned by right understanding until the understanding of no self is very firm. Each moment of understanding, no matter weak or strong, has to arise unexpectedly by conditions, because it is anattā, not in anyone's control.

Attachment is so very tricky. Is there attachment now? It is the cause of dukkha (unsatisfactoriness) and has to be eradicated completely. The idea of self is still there and very strong when understanding has not been developed enough. So there has to be the beginning of understanding of realities as "not self" in order for there to be the development of the right path.

The path has to be dhammatā, "its own way", developing very naturally by conditions.

> *For it does not occur to the eye and visible-datum and so on: 'Would that consciousness might arise from our concurrence.' And they are not active nor do they occupy themselves as door, basis and object for the purpose of arousing consciousness; but rather it is the rule (dhammatā) that eye-consciousness and so on come into being with the concurrence of eye-visible-datum and so on. Therefore they should be regarded as inactive and unoccupied.*
>
> Sammohavinodanī (Dispeller of Delusion) Ch.2, Classification of the Bases, 228 (Translated by L.S. Cousins)

90

Understanding the Nimitta (signs)

Nina asked about understanding and nimitta, the sign of reality. All realities appear as nimitta, but without the paramattha dhammas (absolute realities) there cannot be any nimitta. The nimitta indicates there must be realities arising and falling away rapidly.

Only paññā (understanding) can eradicate attachment little by little, otherwise there is the idea of "I want to understand it". This is wrong. It is a very fine, subtle and difficult way. Paññā has to develop from moment to moment so that the reality can be understood as it is. No one can change the characteristic of hardness or any other reality now when it appears.

Only the realities in this life are taken for Nina or Sujin. All memories of this life will be forgotten in the next life.

If there is the idea of a self existing, whatever we read will be read with the idea of self. In truth there is no self at all. The 4th Noble Truth is the Path. When it is the right Path, there is no doubt anymore about the development of the Path .

No matter how much intellectual understanding there is, if it does not bring any direct awareness now it is useless. There has to be more and more understanding of anattā to condition direct awareness with understanding.

> *"But, venerable sir, how should a bhikkhu know, how should he see, for ignorance to be abandoned by him and true knowledge to arise?"*
>
> *"Here, bhikkhu, a bhikkhu has heard, 'Nothing is worth adhering to.' When a bhikkhu has heard, 'Nothing is worth adhering to,' he directly knows everything. Having directly known everything, he fully understands everything. Having fully understood everything, he sees all signs (nimitta) differently. He sees the eye differently, he sees forms differently... whatever feeling arises with mind-contact as condition... that too he sees differently.*
>
> *"When, bhikkhu, a bhikkhu knows and sees thus, ignorance is abandoned by him and true knowledge arises."*
>
> *Saṃyutta Nikāya 35:80, Abandoning Ignorance (Translated by Bhikkhu Bodhi)*

91

Inner and Outer Realities

In some discussions there were questions about what is meant by internal and external realities in the texts.

There is the worldly or conventional way to talk about "inner and outer", "near and far" and so on but in the absolute sense what is internal and external or near and far? Which cittas, cetasikas and rūpas are being referred to?

For example, what is meant when we read in the Mahā Satipaṭṭhāna Sutta "*Thus he lives contemplating feelings in feelings internally, or he lives contemplating feeling in feelings externally*"?

Usually we think of our own body or feelings as internal and those of others as external. However the truth is much deeper and more subtle. There is no body, there is no self, so what is internal in the Buddha's Teachings?

When we read about any rūpas and other dhammas as being internal or external (ajjhattika or bāhira) they can be understood in two aspects:

1. The rūpas referred to as "my body" are not the same as those referred to as the "other's body", so conventionally it is correct to speak of internal and external rūpas, internal and external vedanā (feelings) and so on.
2. In terms of absolute realities, however, five rūpas are the inner rūpas. These are eye-sense, ear-sense, nose-sense, tongue-sense and body-sense. These are the inner rūpas because without them there cannot be any sense experiencing. The other rūpas are outer rūpas. All cittas are referred to as inner or internal whilst all cetasikas (mental factors) are referred to as outer or external.

For example, at the moment of seeing now, the eye-sense is very close as there is the experiencing of what impinges on it. It is the inner rūpa. The rūpa which appears now, such as that rūpa which is seen, is the outer rūpa. It is far away.

However, at moments of understanding of any of these realities, there are no words, no thoughts of inner or outer. The main point is that there is no one at all. The seeing now is not the same as the other's seeing or the next moment of seeing. In each case, however, it is just seeing, no one's seeing at all.

A citta arises all the time and there must be many cetasikas arising with it. Citta is the "innermost" reality, the chief of experiencing. On its own, the citta is not wholesome or unwholesome. It is pure (paṇḍara) but it is tainted by unwholesome cetasikas. What are usually known are cetasikas and rūpas, not the cittas, the innermost realities.

When the citta is not tainted or disturbed by akusala cetasikas, as well as being paṇḍara (pure), the citta is also pabhassara (radiant or luminous). The bhavaṅga cittas and kusala cittas are said to be radiant because of the cetasikas which arise with them.

The point of study is just to understand what appears now as it is. All dhammas are subtle and it is not the point to know all the details. If the study does not lead to understanding, it is useless.

> *"Luminous, bhikkhus, is this mind, but it is defiled by adventitious defilements."*
>
> *"Luminous, bhikkhus, is this mind, and it is freed from adventitious defilements."*
>
> Aṅguttara Nikāya 1:49, 1:50 Luminous (Translated by Bhikkhu Bodhi)

92

Don't Rush to Understand More!

There needs to be hearing the Teachings, by listening or reading, and careful considering again and again throughout life. It is the only way to eliminate the idea of atta (self). Sacca pāramī (the perfection of truthfulness) means to be truthful about what is known now.

"Don't rush to understand more and more!", Ajahn Sujin reminded the listeners in a Vietnamese discussion. Whatever is to be understood has to be right now. Patience develops with understanding of nāma and rūpa dhammas, those realities which experience an object and those realities which cannot experience anything.

When there is firm understanding of realities there are no questions such as "What can I do?" or "How can I reach this stage?" The understanding develops as a conditioned accumulation.

The Buddha's wisdom and his Teachings are likened to the ocean. What can be discovered deep down in the ocean has to be discovered little by little.

> *The Tathāgata is liberated from reckoning in terms of material form, Vaccha, he is profound, immeasurable, hard to fathom like the ocean.*
>
> *'He reappears' does not apply; 'he does not reappear' does not apply; 'he both reappears and does not reappear' does not apply; 'he neither reappears nor does not reappear' does not apply.*
>
> *The Tathāgata has abandoned that feeling by which one describing the Tathāgata might describe him... has abandoned that perception by which one describing the Tathāgata might describe him... has abandoned those formations by which one describing the Tathāgata might describe him... has abandoned that consciousness by which one describing the Tathāgata might describe him; he has cut it off at the root, made it like a palm stump, done away with it so that it is no longer subject to future arising.*
>
> *The Tathāgata is liberated from reckoning in terms of consciousness, Vaccha; he is profound, immeasurable, hard to fathom like the ocean.*
>
> Majjhima Nikāya 72, Aggivacchagotta Sutta (Translated by Bhikkhu Ñāṇamoli and Bhikkhu Bodhi)

93

Saddhā (confidence)

Nhu Hoa asked about saddhā (confidence) in a Vietnamese discussion. Ajahn Sujin asked her whether citta is now clear and clean. When it is clear and clean there is no lobha (attachment), dosa (aversion) or moha (ignorance). It is saddhā (confidence) which makes it clear and clean.

As a water-clearing gem is said to clear the water, so saddhā cleans the mental states. The more understanding, the more saddhā arises and develops, the more confidence there is in the truth that there is no self.

We have to learn about the realities for there to be conditions for direct awareness. All the realities in life are cittas, cetasikas or rūpas. In the beginning there must be understanding of the difference between those realities which can experience and those realities which are experienced only. Without firm understanding, the various cetasikas such as saddhā, sati (awareness) or viriya (effort) do not appear to be known.

When there is wanting to know and to experience a reality such as saddhā, lobha (attachment) is there. It is so tricky and is always hiding. There will be doubt about anything which appears when there is not enough understanding.

> *Its characteristic is having faith, or its characteristic is trusting. Its function is to clarify, like a water-clearing gem, or its function is to enter into, like the setting out across a flood.*
>
> Visuddhimagga XIV, 140 (Translated by Bhikkhu Ñānamoli)

94

Foot of the World

The subject of the mental factor, vitakka, came up in several discussions. It is usually translated as "thinking", but this may be misleading.

In a sense door process, apart from the moments of seeing, hearing, smelling, tasting or touching, all the other cittas need vitakka to lead the citta and other cetasikas to the object experienced. There is no thinking about a concept yet, but still vitakka has to arise with each of these cittas to experience the sense object.

It seems there is seeing all the time, but it only arises for one moment in the eye-door process. It just sees, arising as vipāka citta (the result of kamma) and falling away instantly. It does not need vitakka. However, the following cittas in the sense-door process are all accompanied by vitakka. It is like "the foot of the world".

In the following mind door processes, vitakka arises with each citta and there is more and more thinking about what has been experienced and remembered by saññā (memory), until there are different ideas of people and things. Without the Buddha's enlightenment we would have no idea.

There is vitakka now but it is not known. Even citta now does not appear. Without the development of understanding of different realities appearing as anattā, there can never be right vitakka (sammā saṅkappa) of the Eightfold Path. When it develops it leads the right understanding, the sammā diṭṭhi, to understand the object experienced clearly.

The Buddha taught about all dhammas in detail, such as how many cetasikas there are and which one is vitakka. Gradually the different functions can be understood.

We learn all these details to let go of the idea of self and the wrong ideas that something can be done or a method followed. We learn that there is no self at all, just different dhammas arising as they are by conditions.

Attachment lurks all the time. It hinders by wanting to know or understand. At any moment of studying the Teachings there has to be understanding that there is no "me", no one at all.

> ***Its [main] characteristic is the lifting of consciousness on to the object; having an object, it (vitakka) lifts consciousness up to it. As someone depending on a relative or friend dear to the king ascends the king's palace, so depending on initial application (vitakka) the mind ascends the object. Therefore it has been said that initial application lifts the mind on to the object.***
> Atthasālinī (The Expositor) 1, Part IV, Ch 1 (Translated by Maung Tin)

95

Deep

When paññā (right understanding) has not been developed, there cannot be the development of the pāramīs, the perfections. There must be the understanding of no self, which is very deep.

Doing good deeds is not enough. Without the understanding of dhammas as anattā, there will be the idea of "my good deeds" all the time.

We had a discussion about how the first mind door process (after a sense door process) always has an image, a nimitta, like a photocopy, of the object experienced in the preceding sense door process. The other mind door processes experience a nimitta of a concept. The seeing consciousness in the sense door process falls away instantly. but there is the idea of a shape, a colour, a thing which is experienced.

The flux of the bhavaṅga (life continuum) cittas is interrupted by sense and mind door processes. As long as the bhavaṅga cittas are arising, nothing appears through a sense or mind doorway, nothing of this world is known.

It is because of the rapidity of the processes, one after the other (with these bhavaṅga cittas in between), that there are conditions for the dhammas to appear as nimittas or signs. It is just like the image of a swirling fire stick or torch.

Right now there is the nimitta of visible object appearing and this is followed by thinking of the shape and form and then the nimitta of a tree or flower or other object. Only the nimitta of a reality, such as the visible object, can be known. We live in the world of nimittas of ideas, dreams and fantasies all the time.

Only the development of right understanding leads to being enlightened to the truth of whatever reality is there now by way of the nimitta. If paññā does not understand the reality, it is impossible for it to understand the attachment to what is conditioned now.

> This dependent arising, Ānanda, is deep and it appears deep. Because of not understanding and not penetrating this Dhamma, Ānanda, this generation has become like a tangled skein, like a knotted ball of thread, like matted rushes and reeds, and does not pass beyond saṃsāra with its plane of misery, unfortunate destinations, and lower realms.
>
> Dīgha Nikāya 15, The Great Discourse on Causation (Translated by Bhikkhu Bodhi)

96

The Good Guy

Lukas started the discussion with a question about good conduct or behaviour (or cariyā in Pāli).

Ajahn Sujin asked him if it is a dhamma and if so which dhamma. Without citta, can there be behaviour?

What is there is not anyone and does not belong to anyone. Usually there is thinking about many ideas. Is it just to learn the details and story of what we have learnt or to understand the truth at this moment? This is the point of understanding, otherwise it is thinking of situations or it is about oneself all the time, even when it is about good behaviour.

Lukas mentioned that people are different and have different accumulations. Not everyone is ready to understand paramattha dhammas (absolute realities). He knows he is supposed to be a "good guy".

> *Ajahn Sujin:* What about being a "good guy" with no understanding?
>
> *Lucas:* They are still reborn in a good realm.
>
> *AS:* What about understanding the truth? Life is in a moment, from life to life. Is it time now to see the value in understanding the truth?

It's so subtle. There is attachment now. Understand the characteristic, there's no thing in it, no one at all. Just a moment and then gone. Understand this to have less clinging to being a "good guy". Who can change conditions for any moment?

If there's understanding of conditions, there will be more conditions to be a "good guy". Without understanding, even though we try and try it will only bring more ignorance and attachment.

Only understanding can condition changing from ignorance to more understanding and better behaviour, not by trying hard.

So the best thing in life is understanding the truth by hearing and considering what is present already by conditions. It cannot bring any sorrow or bad behaviour. In order to have less ignorance and defilements, there must be more understanding of the truth. More understanding leads to more wholesome moments in life.

Later it was stressed that when there is ignorance and attachment there cannot be the "good guy". In truth there is not anyone or anything. It is like the fire which keeps on burning by conditions. Unwholesome cittas are the fire.

> Ajahn Sujin: It doesn't matter what has gone. What about now and now and now!

> *Let not a person revive the past*
> *Or on the future build his hopes;*
> *For the past has been left behind*
> *And the future has not been reached.*
> *Instead with insight let him see*
> *Each presently arisen state;*
> *Let him know that and be sure of it,*
> *Invincibly, unshakeably.*
> *Today Death may come, who knows?*

> *Majjhima Nikāya 131, A Single Excellent Night (Translated by Bhikkhu Ñāṇamoli and Bhikkhu Bodhi)*

4
August 2021

97

What is Hidden?

Nina brought up the topic of the pāramīs (perfections) and the understanding of what is usually hidden all the time.

Ajahn Sujin asked what can be understood. If there are more and more defilements, such as ignorance and attachment, can there be understanding now? This is why the pāramīs are essential to support the development of understanding. Without understanding there is no knowing what is ignorance or what is the danger of other defilements conditioned by ignorance. So all the pāramīs support each other.

Understanding (paññā pāramī) cannot develop without truthfulness (sacca pāramī), courage or effort (viriya pāramī), confidence or determination (adhiṭṭhāna pāramī) and the other pāramīs. When there is understanding there is no idea of "I would like to understand the truth", because there is the understanding that all these dhammas are not self, arising by conditions only.

To understand what is true now, there cannot be clinging to the ideas of "I understand this" or "I have little understanding" and so on. These are all ideas concerning the idea of self.

Nina asked about viriya (effort) to listen. Should there be such effort?

> *Ajahn Sujin:* It doesn't appear so it's the object of doubt and is taken for self. The idea of self is "deep down", like an invisible germ. There is no "should" to be done by a self. Don't try to understand the difference between kusala and akusala, but understand naturally what appears now.

Another friend asked about different tangible objects.

> *AS:* The point is not to try to find out but to understand there is no self. The self lurks at almost every moment.

The ten paramīs are listed in the Buddhavaṃsa of the Khuddaka Nikāya and elaborated on in its commentary, the Cariyāpiṭaka:

1. *Dāna pāramī: generosity*
2. *Sīla pāramī: virtue, morality*
3. *Nekkhama pāramī: renunciation*
4. *Paññā pāramī: understanding*
5. *Viriya pāramī: effort, courage, effort*
6. *Khanti pāramī: patience*
7. *Sacca pāramī: truthfulness*
8. *Adhiṭṭhāna pāramī: determination, resolution*
9. *Mettā pāramī: kindness, friendliness*
10. *Upekkhā pāramī: equanimity.*

5

November 2021

98

Tears

Nina mentioned that the arising and falling away of realities has not been experienced yet.

The truth is that the experience of a moment ago has completely gone. Seeing now is not the seeing of a moment ago, which has completely fallen away. There is nothing, then something then nothing at all. The flux of bhavaṅga (life continuum) cittas is interrupted by sense-door and mind-door processes of cittas all the time. Only paññā, right understanding, can see how worthless each citta is, with no one at all to be found. Each citta arises only once in saṃsāra (the cycle of birth and death). There are just different realities arising by conditions, arising and falling away all the time.

Ajahn Sujin asked Nina where Lodewijk (her deceased husband) is now. There can never be Lodewijk again. It is like that now with regard to each moment of consciousness. We think of this or that dear person, but in truth there are just different realities arising and falling away that we think of as someone. The absolute truth is that there is nobody, only thinking that the person is there. There is nothing other than what appears at this moment.

Nina mentioned that it is hard to reconcile the conventional truth of an existing person with the absolute truth of just different realities arising and falling away. She also wonders how to help others understand.

It is not a matter of "What can I do?" Without understanding the truth intellectually, it is impossible to understand it directly. Right understanding from the beginning is very important. It has to be the understanding of what appears now. When there is hearing, there is no idea about a body or a person. The hearing or any other citta just arises once in saṃsāra.

When there is lobha (attachment), losing what is dear will bring sadness. When there is understanding, it is a relief, a letting go of the burden of clinging at such moments. At such times one lives alone with what is understood, different from the usual clinging to what is dear. In the deepest sense, the world (loka) is that which arises and falls away. No one can do anything.

> *The stream of tears that you have shed as you roamed and wandered through this long course, weeping and wailing because of being united with the disagreeable and separated from the agreeable – this alone is more than the water in the four great oceans. For a long time, bhikkhus, you have experienced the death of a mother; as you have experienced this, weeping and wailing because of being united with the disagreeable and separated from the agreeable, the stream of tears that you have shed is more than the water in the four great oceans.*
>
> *For a long time, bhikkhus, you have experienced the death of a father... brother... sister... son... daughter... the*

> *loss of relatives... the loss of wealth ... loss through illness; as you have experienced this, weeping and wailing because of being united with the disagreeable and separated from the agreeable, the stream of tears that you have shed is more than the water in the four great oceans. For what reason? Because, bhikkhus, this saṃsāra is without discoverable beginning... It is enough to experience revulsion towards all formations, enough to become dispassionate towards them, enough to be liberated from them.*

Saṃyutta Nikāya 15:3, Tears (Translated by Bhikkhu Bodhi)

99

Illumination of the Truth

In a Vietnamese discussion there were some questions about the development of the pāramīs (perfections). Achan Sujin explained that there must be the understanding of what is real now before thinking about the pāramīs. The Buddha said it is so very difficult to penetrate the truth.

Without the understanding of the truth of reality now there cannot be any pāramī, even though there are kusala (wholesome) cittas. The pāramīs develop when there is understanding of what appears little by little. Paññā (understanding) understands what hinders the realisation of the truth about what arises and falls away instantly.

There must be understanding at the intellectual level and sincerity before there can be such direct understanding of the truth.

It has to be the natural way. This means that there is no idea of doing anything by a self in order to understand and be aware of what appears now. Right understanding or wisdom illuminates the truth of what appears.

Tam Tanh asked about vipassanā (insight). Ajahn replied that the answer to all questions is the understanding of the truth now. The truth is that the object is not experienced clearly now. When it is vipassanā understanding, only one reality appears clearly to direct understanding as not self, anattā.

> *Wisdom has the characteristic of penetrating the real specific nature (of dhammas), or the characteristic of sure penetration, like the penetration of an arrow shot by a skillful archer; its function is to illuminate the objective field, like a lamp: its manifestation is non-confusion, like a guide in a forest; concentration, or the four truths, is its proximate cause.*
>
> Commentary to the Cariyāpiṭaka, A Treatise on the Pāramīs (Translated by Bhikkhu Bodhi)

100

Dukkha

Alan suggested that if you understand the cause of dukkha, you will have less attachment.

Ajahn Sujin's response was that if there is no understanding of dhammas as no one, no self, there is no understanding at all. If there is no understanding of what is real now, can there be any understanding of the unsatisfactoriness, dukkha, at the moment of being attached? That which arises and falls is the object of attachment.

Without understanding the danger of what is conditioned to arise and fall away, there must be attachment. If there is not the direct understanding of it arising and falling, it cannot be seen as unsatisfactory and oppressive.

The more understanding there is of reality, the more understanding there is of conditions without naming them. Understanding that seeing now is conditioned does not mean understanding conditions by naming them as kamma condition and so on. There is no time to think about them.

> *Bhikkhus, the eye is impermanent. What is impermanent is suffering. What is suffering is nonself. What*

is nonself should be seen as it really is with correct wisdom thus: 'This is not mine, this I am not, this is not my self.'

The ear is impermanent... The nose is impermanent... The tongue is impermanent... The body is impermanent... The mind is impermanent. What is impermanent is suffering. What is suffering is nonself. What is nonself should be seen as it really is with correct wisdom thus: 'This is not mine, this I am not, this is not my self.'

Saṃyutta Nikāya 35:1, The Internal as Impermanent (Translated by Bhikkhu Bodhi)

101

Clear Understanding

Nina asked about the distinction between intellectual understanding and direct understanding.

There cannot be direct understanding unless the reality appearing is understood as just a dhamma. Body consciousness experiences hardness now, not a leg or a table as we are used to thinking. Without direct understanding when such realities appear, they cannot appear well.

Without the understanding of realities well, there cannot be the arising of the vipassanā ñāṇas (clear insight understanding) which is deeper still. The various nāmas and rūpas appear clearly and distinctly through the mind door, one after another at moments of vipassanā ñāṇa.

In between the vipassanā ñāṇas there are the pariññās, the realisations that what has been clearly understood apply to other realities in daily life.

At the second stage of insight, there is the understanding of the conditioned nature of realities. There is no naming of different conditions because that is just the story. No matter what arises and when, it is not by a self. Each dhamma has its proper conditions to arise.

We read about how people who have not become enlightened to the truth, delight in the earth element and every other kind of conditioned reality, taking each one for self, or for some thing, in various ways. The texts indicate the reason for this:

> **What is the reason? Because it has not been fully understood by him, I declare.**
> Majjhima Nikāya 1, The Discourse on the Root of Existence (Translated by Bhikkhu Bodhi)

6
December 2021

102

The Masterpiece

Maeve mentioned that when hearing the sound of a voice, there is familiarity with something unique when one recognises that voice.

We discussed that the sound that was heard a moment ago has gone. There is just the shadow of it now. Each sound only ever arose once and has gone completely. There is just a moment of hearing followed by countless other moments in rapid succession.

It is like looking at a dot on a piece of paper. When there are so many dots, we recognise the shape and form as a cat or a dog or other object. It is like the circle of lights or fire created by a magician or the waving of a sparkler. However, the cittas arise and fall away much more rapidly. What is experienced is the nimitta, the sign, of each reality from one process to another.

The paṭisandhi citta (birth consciousness) and all the bhavaṅga cittas (life continuum cittas) are conditioned by the same past kamma, so there is the stream of consciousness known as this or that personality just for this life until death. This gives the illusion of something unique which is ever present.

Saññā (memory) passes on what has been remembered by anantara (proximity) and samanantara (contiguity) conditions. One citta follows another instantly from moment to moment, life to life and the citta which follows has to be the way it is conditioned to be. By these conditions, each cuti citta (death consciousness) has to be immediately followed by a paṭisandhi citta.

> *How is consciousness (i.e., mind) capable of producing a variety or diversity of effects in action? There is no art in the world more variegated than the art of painting. In painting, the painter's masterpiece is more artistic than the rest of his pictures. An artistic design occurs to the painters of masterpieces that such and such pictures should be drawn in such and such a way. Through this artistic design there arise operations of the mind (or artistic operations) accomplishing such things as sketching the outline, putting on the paint, touching up, and embellishing. Then in the picture known as the masterpiece is effected a certain (central) artistic figure. Then the remaining portion of the picture is completed by the work of planning in mind as, 'Above this figure let this be; underneath, this; on both sides, this.'*
>
> *Thus all classes of arts in the world, specific or generic, are achieved by the mind. And owing to its capacity thus to produce a variety or diversity of effects in action, the mind, which achieves all these arts, is itself artistic like the arts themselves. Nay, it is even more artistic than the art itself, because the latter cannot execute every design perfectly. For that reason the Blessed One has said, 'Bhikkhus, have you seen a masterpiece of painting?' 'Yea, Lord.' 'Bhikkhus, that masterpiece of art is designed by the mind. Indeed, Bhikkhus, the mind is even more artistic than that masterpiece.'*

Atthasālinī (The Expositor) I, Part II, Ch I (Translated by Pe Maung Tin)

103

The Result of Kamma

Joanne asked a question in a Chinese discussion about the results of kamma. One person may experience a pleasant object but another may experience an unpleasant object. One person may feel hot whilst another may feel cold in the same situation, for example.

However, can anyone distinguish between pleasant and unpleasant objects? We just judge them by our reactions to the objects. Why would we like to know whether the experiencing of such objects is the result of good or bad kamma? Usually it is because it is "I" who would like to know.

Seeing now arises, experiences its object and falls away immediately. It is impossible to know whether a pleasant or unpleasant object was experienced at that instant.

It is much more useful to understand this moment as not self rather than trying to know whether the object that has gone was pleasant or unpleasant. It is only thinking and speculating about realities that have gone. It can only be known whether there is pleasant or unpleasant feeling with regard to the tangible object experienced now. However, even the feeling is difficult to know, so can the object which conditions it be known?

There is nothing but that which experiences and that which is experienced. The absolute reality is just at this moment of consciousness. There is just a moment of seeing and then it has gone. The same is true of the bodily experience. The absolute truth is that there is no head, no arms, no eyes or anything else. These are ideas, concepts only.

Vincent asked about a baby born with two hearts. However, no matter whether there is a body with two heads or two hearts, there are only rūpas conditioned by kamma to arise and fall away. There is no one, no thing, only one object experienced. As long as there is still the idea of something existing there cannot be the understanding of no self.

Da Zhuang also asked about conjoined twins and shared kamma. Each lifestream of cittas experiences the results of different kammas. It may seem that the results are shared, but seeing now, hearing now and other results of kamma are never shared.

> Bhikkhus, there are these four inconceivable matters that one should not try to conceive; one who tries to conceive them would reap either madness or frustration. What four? (1) The domain of the Buddhas is an inconceivable matter... (2) The domain of one in jhāna is an inconceivable matter... (3) The result of kamma is an inconceivable matter... (4) Speculation about the world is an inconceivable matter...
>
> Aṅguttara Nikāya 4:77, Inconceivable Matters (Translated by Bhikkhu Bodhi)

104

The End of Saṃsāra

Joanne asked questions about what she could do in this life and about the end of saṃsāra (the cycle of birth and death).

It was explained that there is no one at all. If this is not understood, it is always the study of the Teachings with the idea of "I". There has to be the learning about the truth which is hidden.

> *Ajahn Sujin:* Why does one want to be out of saṃsāra?
>
> *Joanne:* Because of dukkha and because the Buddha encouraged it.
>
> *AS:* Who knows about the truth of dukkha now? Is it better to know what avijjā (ignorance) is now or just try to go out of saṃsāra?

Jo: To be away from avijjā.

AS: So we cannot say there is enough understanding of dukkha. For the ordinary person it's just unpleasant feeling (which is known). Would you like to be away from pleasant feeling?

Jo: No

AS: So, not out of saṃsāra yet. Without seeing, hearing, smelling, tasting and touching how is there pleasant feeling? The Buddha said attachment is the 2nd Noble Truth, the cause of dukkha, which should be eradicated. If there is not yet the understanding of dukkha, the arising and falling away at this moment, it's useless to dream about getting away from saṃsāra.

It is just "I" who wants the "I" to be happy with pleasant feeling all the time, not the understanding that the pleasant feeling lasts for a very short moment, that it is anattā, arising and falling away.

So see the benefit of understanding the truth of reality. Just live to understand dhammas. As long as paññā (understanding) doesn't directly understand lobha (attachment), it can never understand the danger of lobha and lead out of saṃsāra.

In other words, the understanding has to develop to realise the Four Noble Truths.

> *In the ultimate sense all the truths should be understood as void because of the absence of (i) any experiencer, (ii) any doer, (iii) anyone who is extinguished, and (iv) any goer. Hence this is said:*

> *'For there is suffering, but none who suffers;*
> *Doing exists although there is no doer;*
> *Extinction is but no extinguished person;*
> *Although there is a path, there is no goer'.*

Visuddhimagga XVI, 90 (Translated by Bhikkhu Ñāṇamoli)

105

The 3 Gocaras (1)

In a Vietnamese discussion we discussed more about the levels of understanding referred to in the Visuddhimagga and in other texts as upanissaya gocara, ārakkhā gocara and upanibhanda gocara. Gocara here (literal meaning 'resort') refers to the reality which is experienced by right understanding.

Understanding of any object appearing has to develop on and on. For example, visible object is experienced, but without understanding, it is just the object of attachment as usual. If there is intellectual understanding about it, there is the beginning of understanding the truth and this will lead to seeing the benefit of understanding it more and more. By upanissaya gocara, it will become the habit to understand it.

From the very beginning there has to be the understanding that nothing can be taken for any thing or person. This leads to more confidence in the truth of any object. The accumulation of the idea of self has been the habit for so very long. When it is upanissaya gocara, there is the understanding of which objects can be known without any selection at all. All dhammas are uncontrollable.

Ārakkhā gocara is the protection from the arising of akusala (unwholesome) cittas through the right understanding of different realities from the development of upanissaya gocara. The right understanding becomes the 'protection' against the continual arising of lobha (attachment), enjoying one's akusala again and again. What we cling to has already gone. With the growth of understanding there is the gradual letting go of clinging to conditioned dhammas which cannot be controlled at all. Whilst kusala cittas are better than akusala, without understanding, they too just become the object for more clinging.

It is by wise considering that paññā can grow to see that there is no one who can control anything and there is ārakkhā, protection, from the wrong idea of trying to get rid of lobha (attachment) instead of understanding it as not self. Other kinds of kusala cannot protect one from wrong understanding.

No matter whether the cittas now are akusala or kusala, paññā can understand them as anattā. It is understanding of this level which will condition upanibandha gocara. This is the direct understanding of the truth of different realities. There is no doubt about what has to be developed.

The development is slow but it is the right way. There is not anyone who can try to make it arise or develop. Without understanding there cannot even be upanissaya gocara because it is the Teaching of the Buddha. Every day is the test and proof of understanding.

> *What is (proper) resort as anchoring (upanibandha gocara)? It is the four foundations of mindfulness on which the mind is anchored; for this is said by the Blessed One: 'Bhikkhus, what is a bhikkhu's resort, his own native place? It is these four foundations of mindfulness'. This is called (proper) resort as anchoring.*
>
> Visuddhimagga I, 51 (Translated by Bhikkhu Ñāṇamoli)

106

Āyūhana

Sundara read passages relating to āyūhana in the Visuddhimagga and asked questions about them.

Āyūhana refers to the collection of past kamma which conditioned rebirth and which conditions other results in the present life. It is a very deep topic.

Ajahn Sujin asked him whether it was just the study of the words or the truth of the words. There has to be the understanding of dhammas as not self. "Read any word just to understand what is there now by conditions." It is understanding which gradually lets go of clinging to other subjects to be known.

The kamma which conditions the last javana cittas before death brings results by way of the next birth and during the next lifetime. Other kammas which have been accumulated can also bring results in that lifetime. These kammas are what āyūhana refers to. They can be from the previous life or from aeons and aeons ago.

There was a further question about how āyūhana relates to birth in a life.

Birth consciousness (paṭisandhi citta) is so very different according to whether it is the result of kusala kamma or akusala kamma. The kamma which conditions the paṭisandhi citta conditions further vipāka cittas and rūpas during that life. Other kammas accumulated in the past can also bring results during that life. For example, human life is the result of kusala kamma, a pleasant result, but one can be healthy or unhealthy, rich or poor and so on. A dog may have strong health while a wealthy person may have poor health.

Āyūhana refers to all these kammas bringing results in that life.

> *In the previous kamma-process becoming, there is delusion, which is* ignorance; *there is accumulation[s] (āyūhana), which is* [kamma]; *there is attachment, which is* craving; *there is embracing, which is* clinging; *there is volition, which is* becoming; *thus these five things in the previous kamma-process becoming are conditions for rebirth-linking here [in the present becoming].*
>
> Visuddhimagga XVII, 292 (Translated by Bhikkhu Ñāṇamoli)

107

The 3 Gocaras (2)

There was further discussion on this deep topic.

Upanissaya (habitual) gocara is the reality experienced which has become the habitual object of understanding. The object of understanding taught by the Buddha must be different because it is the object which is understood as not self, not some thing. It has to be an absolute reality, not a concept. When there is no familiarity with the reality as it is, it cannot be upanissaya gocara.

The object of the understanding which has developed further is ārakkhā (protection) gocara. There is protection at such moments from what is wrong and harmful, such as the usual attachments. Sati (awareness) arises with it to guard against these states arising.

Now, are there the ordinary ideas thought about, or is there some understanding of the truth developing gradually about the reality appearing now? There should be no expectation, but gradually there can be more understanding of the truth that what is experienced is anattā, no self, no thing to be found. This is ārakkhā gocara. It protects from having attachment again and again, enjoying one's wholesome and unwholesome states of mind. Whatever arises cannot be controlled at all. If understanding is not strong enough, there will not be this protection.

It is impossible to hurry to understand the object appearing now, such as what is visible or the sound heard. Now is the test of whether the understanding is strong enough to understand realities and to condition ārakkhā gocara which sees the disadvantages of unwholesome states at different levels.

Even arahats have cittas which arise without understanding, but for them no akusala (unwholesome states) arise. If there is not the continued development of the understanding of the various realities, there cannot be the upanibandha gocara, the anchoring with direct understanding to the object. It is not enough just to have understanding of the rūpas that are experienced, there must be the understanding of the realities which experience them too. The realities are very close now. This moment is the test of how much understanding there is.

Upanibandha is like the anchor of a ship. The ship does not move. In the same way the understanding is "fixed" to the object appearing. The cittas do not drift along with the current of defilements. There is no thought about another object at such moments. Just one reality can appear at a time for an instant only.

> *Suppose, bhikkhus, there was a seafaring ship bound with rigging that had been worn away in the water for six months. It would be hauled up on dry land during the cold season and its rigging would be further attacked by wind and sun. Inundated by rain from a rain cloud, the rigging would easily collapse and rot away. So too, bhikkhus, when a bhikkhu dwells devoted to development, his fetters easily collapse and rot away.*
>
> Saṃyutta Nikāya 22:101, The Ship (Translated by Bhikkhu Bodhi)

108

Anger

There were some discussions about anger.

When there is a lot of anger, there can still be consideration with understanding that it is anattā (not self), conditioned to be that way.

It is useless to keep hurting oneself. No one can harm you, no matter what they may say or do. Only one's own dosa (aversion) hurts. It is not "mine" and it has gone instantly. Everything is gone, all gone from moment to moment.

The truth is that each dhamma falls away from moment to moment. Yesterday was yesterday, completely gone. Now will be yesterday so very soon. So just live to understand the truth which is the best thing in life.

One may be afraid of akusala, such as anger, but when paññā is there, there is no fear of anything. What you are afraid of has fallen away already.

What does one get angry about? In truth it is just about what is seen or heard for an instant and thought about. There is no one there to be angry with. It is just the ignorance which takes it for something or someone that is so important to be angry with. There is just anger again and again with what has already gone away. There is nothing to be angry with.

> *'What do you think, brahmin? Do your friends and colleagues, kinsmen and relatives, as well as guests come to visit you?'*
>
> *'Sometimes they come to visit, Master Gotama.'*
>
> *'Do you then offer them some food or a meal or a snack?'*
>
> *'Sometimes I do, Master Gotama.'*
>
> *'But if they do not accept it from you, then to whom does the food belong?'*
>
> *'If they do not accept it from me, then the food still belongs to us.'*
>
> *'So too, brahmin, we — who do not abuse anyone, who do not scold anyone, who do not rail against anyone — refuse to accept from you the abuse and scolding and tirade you let loose at us. It still belongs to you, brahmin! It still belongs to you, brahmin!'* ...
>
> *One who repays an angry man with anger*
> *Thereby makes things worse for himself.*
> *Not repaying an angry man with anger,*
> *One wins a battle hard to win."*
>
> Saṃyutta Nikāya 7:2, Abuse (Translated by Bhikkhu Bodhi)

109

Passing Away

A friend's husband, Charoen, had very recently passed away. He was fortunate to have had a keen interest in the Dhamma in this life. Now he is a "new person", no more being Charoen. In his next life, there is no remembrance of Charoen and his past life, just as we have no memory of our past life.

In truth, reality changes from moment to moment and just as there is no "me", there never was Charoen in reality. There is only ever the flux of whatever arises and falls away, covering up the truth.

There is no need to be sad at all about the passing away of a dear one. It is so very ordinary. Just do good deeds for that one or any others to appreciate. This is the best for anyone who has passed away. There is no need to keep hurting oneself by grieving and feeling sad. It is just one's akusala (unwholesome states) that keeps hurting oneself again and again.

What use is it to feel sorry for the dear ones not to be in this life anymore? They may be in a happier plane of existence. They are unlikely to have any recollection of their past lives. For us, whatever seems very important now will soon be forgotten. Even the thinking about the dear ones has all gone, along with the seeing, hearing and other experiences.

When it is understood that there is no one there, life gradually becomes easier. Just understand the truth little by little. It takes a long time to just understand a reality now.

Without avijjā (ignorance) in the past, there could not have been past kusala or akusala kamma and there could not be the present life. The understanding of conditioned dhammas has to develop until it is clear that there is no one here or there at all. After each moment of seeing, there is thinking which is conditioned to think about what was seen. Because of ignorance and wrong understanding it is taken for something or someone instantly.

Instead of memories about this or that person, this or that situation, gradually there can be more memory with understanding to think about the truth at any time. This will save one from having more unwholesome thoughts very gradually, little by little. It is against the current of ignorance to understand the truth.

Whatever occurred has all gone and it is useless to try to find out what has gone. Only the present dhammas (realities) can be known. There has to be the letting go of whatever there is in life. No one can force it, but understanding can develop little by little that there are only dhammas, no people at all. All are anattā (not self).

The following are the verses spoken by the father (the Bodhisatta) and then the mother when their son was killed by a snake. For them, life carried on as usual:

> *"Man quits his mortal frame, when joy in life is past.*
> *Even as a snake is wont its worn out slough to cast.*
> *No friends' lament can touch the ashes of the dead.*
> *Why should I grieve? He fares the way he had to tread.*
>
> *Uncalled he hither came, unbidden soon to go.*
> *Even as he came he went, what cause is here for woe?*
> *No friends' lament can touch the ashes of the dead.*
> *Why should I grieve? He fares the way he had to tread.*
>
> Jātaka 354, Uraga Jātaka (Translated by E.B. Cowell)

110

Wrong Practice

Pal and other friends asked about wrong practice, using the Pāli term, sīlabbataparāmāsa.

> *Ajahn Sujin:* Understanding doesn't depend on the word used but on the understanding of the truth of what appears now as not self. Any kind of akusala is here now. Should it not be known as not self rather than

trying to find out whether it's sīlabbataparāmāsa? Have there not been all kinds of akusala from morning until now? Have any of them been known as realities which are now gone? What is trying to know the meaning of sīlabbataparāmāsa now? Can it bring any understanding of the truth?

Any word we use to represent reality cannot be the understanding of the truth because it is just thinking about the term. What about when we are satisfied with the meaning? Is it the same as the understanding of what appears as not self? Should any reality now be known or should we just keep thinking of different terms? What motivates such interest in different terms? What reality is it that keeps motivating questions about what this and that are endlessly, not just about sīlabbataparāmāsa?

Pal: Lobha

From waking up until now there is lobha, attachment. If it is not known as not self, it is there again and again. Understanding the reality, such as when thinking about sīlabbataparāmāsa, is the only way to eradicate the wrong practice. This is far more useful than just thinking about different situations and wondering if wrong practice is arising at such times.

Anyone who has not reached the first stage of enlightenment is bound to have conditions for wrong practice and the wrong understanding of self. Understanding the truth at the present moment is more useful than trying to work out what the Buddha said about this or that word or about this or that situation. Otherwise there will just be conditions to think on and on endlessly about the term.

Ajahn Sujin: Anattā is the truth of all kinds of realities in life now.

The absolute truth can never be changed. We can have ideas about whether it is true or not but what is the absolute truth? We try to make decisions about what is right but usually this is without any understanding.

The truth cannot be changed. There has to be the direct realization, not just the belief in what has been heard. The understanding has to develop at this very moment.

Questions about "how did I do?", "what shall I do?" or "how am I doing?" are not questions about the truth at the present moment. The Buddha did not tell his listeners what they should or should not do because each reality is conditioned, each way of behaviour is according to accumulated tendencies and there is no one to do anything.

If there is no interest and understanding of the truth, in ignorance there is the taking of seeing and hearing now for "I see", "I hear" and ideas about following particular practices.

> *Ajahn Sujin*: There is so much to learn, not by the word but by considering little by little. Understand what is there because it's very close.

> **This is how he attends unwisely: 'Was I in the past? Was I not in the past? What was I in the past? How was I in the past? Having been what, what did I become in the past? Shall I be in the future? Shall I not be in the future? What shall I be in the future? How shall I be in the future? Having been what, what shall I become in the future?'**
> **Or else he is inwardly perplexed about the present thus: 'Am I? Am I not? What am I? How am I? Where has this being come from? Where will it go?'**
> Majjhima Nikāya 62, All the Taints (Translated by Bhikkhu Ñāṇamoli and Bhikkhu Bodhi)

7

January 2022

111

Citta is Paṇḍara (pure)

In a Vietnamese discussion, Lan raised helpful questions about the nature of cittas and cetasikas. We considered why cittas are paṇḍara (pure) but cetasikas are not. This is a deep and subtle topic.

There has to be more understanding about the difference between cittas and cetasikas. For example, now at a moment of seeing, can anyone understand the difference between the citta and accompanying cetasikas that arise together? Only paññā can understand the reality which is the chief in experiencing the object as different from the cetasikas, the mental factors which accompany it. Without understanding the nature of citta there cannot be the understanding that it is seeing consciousness which sees, not someone who sees now. Likewise, at a moment of hearing, there is no one who hears, just hearing consciousness which hears what is heard. Because of ignorance, the citta is taken for "I who sees" or "I who hears".

From birth to death there is the reality which arises and is the chief in experiencing the object. It is different from the attachment which likes the object or the aversion which dislikes the object or any other cetasika which performs its own particular function.

Only citta is paṇḍara (pure). It does not like or dislike anything. It just arises to experience the object. Each citta is paṇḍara regardless of whether it arises with kusala or akusala cetasikas. At the moment akusala cetasikas arise, only the citta is paṇḍara. The akusala cetasikas cannot change the nature of citta as the chief or leader in experiencing the object clearly. This is true from birth to death. It always experiences the object clearly, without like or dislike. When the citta arises with paññā (right understanding), the citta is paṇḍara, experiencing the object clearly, but it doesn't understand anything. It never performs the functions of any of the accompanying cetasikas.

Understanding this is not a matter of just repeating the term paṇḍara, but beginning to understand the nature of citta, no matter whether it arises with kusala or akusala cetasikas or when there is a resultant citta, such as at a moment of seeing or hearing.

Is there understanding now of whatever appears as not self? It needs the words of the Buddha to understand the different realities, to understand the difference between cittas and cetasikas but not by just remembering or repeating the words.

Lan asked whether it is right to say that citta is poisoned or tainted by akusala cetasikas. The citta with attachment is not the same as the citta with aversion or with understanding. Even though the citta just has the function of clearly experiencing the object and this cannot be changed, the citta and cetasikas arise together and condition each other.

It should be noted that the meaning of paṇḍara is different from pabhassara (luminous). When the citta is akusala it cannot be pabhassara even though it is paṇḍara. However at moments of akusala vipāka, the result of akusala kamma, the cittas are pabhassara because no akusala cetasikas arise with them. This is why it is said that all bhavaṅga cittas (life continuum consciousness) are pabhassara.

> Mind also is said to be 'clear' (paṇḍara) in the sense of 'exceedingly pure,' with reference to the life-continuum (bhavaṅga citta).
> So the Buddha has said: 'Bhikkhus, the mind is luminous (pabhassara), but is corrupted by adventitious corruptions.'
> Though immoral (akusala), it is called 'clear' (paṇḍara) because it issues [from bhavaṅga citta], just as a tributary of the Ganges is like the Ganges and a tributary of the Godhāvarī is like the Godhāvarī.

Atthasālinī (The Expositor) I, Part II, Ch II (Translated by Pe Maung Tin)

112

The Abhidhamma is Now

Nina asked for an example of māna (conceit) that commonly arises now.

Ajahn Sujin: What do you think about "me, me, me"?

If māna appears it can be the object of direct understanding. The anattā characteristic of different realities has to show up more and more until all kinds of realities are seen clearly.

Paññā (right understanding) is a condition by way of natural decisive support condition for all kinds of wholesome states. Now unwholesome states of one kind or another strongly bind to the object. When there is direct understanding, it binds to the object with wholesome cittas rooted in understanding. At such moments there are no conditions for such thinking about "me" or various situations, taking them for being real.

There has to be the understanding not just of the object experienced but also that which experiences the object. This is the only way to understand the nature of anattā. For example, not just visible object has to be understood as what is seen, but also the seeing consciousness, the citta, has to be understood as just the reality which sees. Otherwise there will be the idea of "my seeing" again and again.

Tadao asked a question about the realities experienced now.

> *Ajahn Sujin:* What appears now?
>
> *Tadao:* A computer
>
> *AS:* What is true is that different colours are seen, only one at a time. That which is seen is arising and falling away so rapidly that it hides the truth of everything.

Citta is like a magician. It seems that many objects appear together, but in fact only one object is experienced at a time.

The absolute truth was discovered by the Buddha. Because of the rapid arising and falling away of realities there is the idea of a self all the time, but this is an illusion. The truth is so very subtle. Only one reality at a time can be known. The wisdom of the Buddha can begin to be known from the understanding of his Teachings.

Each of the seven books of the Abhidhamma (and all the other Teachings) are about the truth of the present moment.

> *Consciousness is like a magical illusion (māyā) in the sense that it is insubstantial and cannot be grasped. Consciousness is even more transient and fleeting than a magical illusion. For it gives the impression that a person comes and goes, stands and sits, with the same mind, but the mind is different in each of these activities. Consciousness deceives the multitude like a magical illusion.*
>
> Commentary to Saṃyutta Nikāya 22:95, "A Lump of Foam" (Translated by Bhikkhu Bodhi)

113

Falling Down

Nina mentioned she had fallen down in a shopping mall recently and she continues to think about the incident and the pain.

Ajahn Sujin: Forget about it! Is it there now?

Now is not the moment of falling down, it is never the same moment, never the same reality which has fallen away.

Nina: I find it so important, by conditions.

AS: What about now? Otherwise it can't be understood. This is the world.

Memory conditions thinking about how "I feel" and "what happened to me" but there is no one at all. Whatever appears is to be understood. There is clinging to "me" and "my existence" all the time.

Nina also mentioned that her niece is very sad because her husband has left her. She misses him a lot. Everything has to change, however. It is the time to understand the truth. She can be friendly to him or anyone, she can do good with no sorrow or regret. Even if he had not left now, what about when death comes? Whether it is death or he has left her, it is all by conditions.

Life must be the separation from everything we hold dear. We hope for this and that but life is bound to be different from what we wish for. When death comes, where is one's husband or friend? It is just one's own clinging. We should be wise to the way life is. There is clinging all the time to different situations, not letting go and not understanding the truth now.

When feeling angry or disappointed, one just hurts oneself and feels sad instead of taking care with understanding and wholesome cittas. We can have good will and understanding for others, instead of love and clinging. It is just our own habit of clinging which conditions so much grief. No one else can hurt us at all, no one, but we are used to blaming others. What was seen has completely gone. No matter how mean or selfish someone might have been, that is their accumulation. One's own accumulation of unwholesomeness keeps harming oneself, but the kind thoughts and understanding never harm. The best way is to be friendly, to forgive and not to regret anything. Such events can be the teacher. When there is understanding, there is no regret at all.

If there is no clinging to oneself, there cannot be clinging to the other person. The less clinging, the more happily one lives without regret or blame. When doing good deeds one forgets about the problem or the other's bad deeds. There is less time to think about such difficulties.

The absolute truth is that life is just in a moment. Understanding this one does not care what the next moment will be. It will be by conditions like now. To live the best way is to understand the truth of life as it is, the arising and falling away of life now.

> **Drawing in the mind's thoughts**
> *As a tortoise draws its limbs into its shell,*
> ***Independent [of craving and views], not harassing others,***
>   ***fully quenched [of defilements],***
> *A bhikkhu would not blame anyone.*

Saṃyutta Nikāya 1:17, Difficult to Practise (Translated by Bhikkhu Bodhi)

February 2022

114

Kamma and Birth

There was a discussion about kamma conditioning birth. In the past there have been so many kammas which can produce results, but only one kamma conditions the citta which performs the function of birth, the paṭisandhi citta. After that, the same kamma will condition bhavaṅga (life-continuum) cittas and other vipāka (result) cittas during life as well as the cuti (death) citta at the end of life.

Other past kammas, kusala and akusala, will bring other results during life too. The moments of seeing, hearing, smelling, tasting and touching now in daily life are all examples of vipāka cittas conditioned by past kamma. There are supporting or impeding kinds of kamma. For example, only unpleasant objects can be experienced when impeding akusala kamma brings its results. There can be a sudden death when a life ends prematurely, but it is always kamma which conditions death at the time of an accident or any other occurrence.

Birth in the human realm is the result of kusala kamma. It cannot be known what kamma conditioned it. It may have been from aeons and aeons ago. The results now may be the result of kamma from countless lifetimes ago, last life or this life. No one knows.

The object of the paṭisandhi (birth) citta is the same as that of the bhavaṅga (life continuum) cittas which follow and the cuti (death) consciousness at the end of life. That object is unknown now and the object of these cittas in the next life will also be unknown.

Rather than trying to work out the intricacies of kamma or speculate on what kamma produced what result, it is much more beneficial to understand the reality experienced now as not self.

> **The result of kamma is an inconceivable matter that one should not try to conceive; one who tries to conceive it would reap either madness or frustration.**
>
> Aṅguttara Nikāya, 4:77 Inconceivable Matters (Translated by Bhikkhu Bodhi)

115

Fire! (1)

Leena and Nina asked what is meant when it is said in the suttas that one should develop or practise as if one's head is on fire and that all conditioned dhammas are burning with the fire of attachment, aversion and ignorance.

Usually the defilements are taken for being one's own, and there is more and more clinging, wishing and wanting of all kinds. There is no understanding what the fire is, even when we are addicted to it, like a moth attracted to a flame.

If this moment were permanent as we would like it to be, there would be no fire at all. It seems so pleasant but it has gone instantly.

There is more and more desire for that object which is burning. Without the desire, there would be no trouble, no burning at all. At the moment when the reality is taken for self or belonging to self, there is the fire of ignorance, attachment and aversion which follows. They are there all the time unknown. There is ignorance of that which burns up all the time because there is the idea of self and there is so much clinging from birth to death.

Without defilements there is no more birth, no unpleasant moments, no difficulties, no fire at all. These defilements are so very "thick and sticky", however.

The arising and falling away of realities do not appear to clear understanding, so the fire is not understood as being very dangerous. There is just clinging to one object after another. We think we live happily but death can come at any time, loss can come at any time.

Only when nothing arises will there be no more seeing, hearing and so on, no more ideas that "I see" or "I hear" or clinging of any kind in life. So there needs to be the learning to live with understanding of the truth. This means not selecting or choosing what will arise or be known, but understanding that whatever arises does so by conditions and falls away instantly. The understanding has to be very natural, not with an idea of "I can develop" or "I can practise".

After learning the truth about how all conditioned dhammas are burning with attachment, aversion and ignorance, the Buddha said:

> *Bhikkhus, all is burning. And what, bhikkhus, is the all that is burning? The eye is burning, forms are burning, eye-consciousness is burning, eye-contact is burning, and whatever feeling arises with eye-contact as condition — whether pleasant or painful or neither-painful-nor-pleasant- that too is burning. Burning with what? Burning with the fire of lust, with the fire of hatred, with the fire of delusion; burning with birth, aging, and death; with sorrow, lamentation, pain, displeasure, and despair, I say.*

Chapter 8. February 2022

> *The ear is burning... The mind is burning... and whatever feeling arises with mind-contact as condition—whether pleasant or painful or neither-painful-nor-pleasant—that too is burning. Burning with what? Burning with the fire of lust, with the fire of hatred, with the fire of delusion; burning with birth, aging, and death; with sorrow, lamentation, pain, displeasure, and despair, I say.*
>
> Saṃyutta Nikāya 35:28, Burning (Translated by Bhikkhu Bodhi)

9
April 2022

116

Fire! (2)

Azita helpfully brought up the topic of Fire again.

Ajahn Sujin stressed that when fire is far away it does not hurt but when it is close, "on one's head", what will one do? Ignorance is like a fire. Without it, there is no fire. When it is on one's head, there is no understanding of what is present, no understanding of the truth. Ignorance is more dangerous than any fire.

So we can consider the "far fire" and the "near fire". The danger of the near fire is that it keeps on burning until the end of life. The various realities keep on arising and falling away and usually no one experiences the truth. They are likened to a fire for those who understand them as impermanent dhammas which are anattā.

What is the use of seeing, hearing and all other experiences arising and falling away until death? The world is breaking up all the time. When there is right understanding of the close fire, would anyone like to continue with the experiencing of realities arising and falling away by conditions, life to life? There is the understanding of the fire on one's head when there is the understanding of the danger of ignorance.

No one is disturbed now by seeing, hearing and thinking and the taking of what is experienced for something or some person. However, what is the use of thinking with ignorance again and again? It is like watching a play which is so enticing but then comes to an end. Life is like this before death, so captivating and then gone. In truth nothing is there, no one is there, each reality has gone. Only right understanding can realise the truth.

The danger of the fire is only fully realised at the stage of bhaya vipassanā ñāṇa, the sixth stage of insight. This is the direct knowledge of the danger and fearfulness of all conditioned realities. It is understood that whatever is conditioned is "fire on one's head". The danger is much more apparent at this stage. The world is ablaze because of the inherent nature of realities to arise and fall away.

> *And what, bhikkhus, is the Dhamma exposition on the theme of burning? It would be better, bhikkhus, for the eye faculty to be lacerated by a red-hot iron pin burning, blazing, and glowing, than for one to grasp the sign through the features in a form cognizable by the eye...*
>
> *In regard to this, bhikkhus, the instructed noble disciple reflects thus: 'Leave off lacerating the eye faculty with a red-hot iron pin burning, blazing, and glowing. Let me attend only to this: So the eye is impermanent, forms are impermanent, eye-consciousness is impermanent, eye-contact is impermanent, whatever feeling arises with eye-contact as condition — whether pleasant or painful or neither-painful-nor-pleasant — that too is impermanent.'*

Saṃyutta Nikāya 35:235, The Exposition on Burning (Translated by Bhikkhu Bodhi)

117

Kusala and Akusala Sīla

Carmen brought up the topic of following rules of behaviour and sīla (morality).

People usually study the story of sīla instead of understanding the truth at this moment. Without the Buddha's Teachings it would be impossible to understand that there is no one who behaves well or badly. What is most important is to understand what appears now for an instant.

In the deepest sense, sīla is not just what we are used to taking for our behaviour. It is the behaviour of the citta (consciousness) which experiences an object. The behaviour of the citta arises and falls away at each moment, no matter whether we are talking about a person, a cat, a dog or an insect. Different conditioned realities arise and fall away unexpectedly all the time.

If there were no cittas and cetasikas, there would be no sīla, no kusala (wholesome) sīla and no akusala (unwholesome) sīla. Cittas and cetasikas which are wholesome are kusala sīla no matter whether there is kindness, generosity, samatha (calm) or moments of satipaṭṭhāna (direct awareness and understanding of realities). The highest level of sīla is adhi-sīla. Generosity (dāna) is kusala sīla but it is not adhi-sīla (higher sīla) because there is no direct understanding of the reality at such moments. Whenever the the cittas and cetasikas are unwholesome, it is akusala sīla, no matter what the outer appearance of an act may be.

Jotika mentioned that a friend wished to help a dog which was in pain and dying. She did not want to kill the dog but found it a difficult situation.

Ajahn Sujin asked if the dog might die before she tried to kill it. What if the dog died first or what if she tried to kill it but it did not die? It all depends on conditions at each moment. What about the citta that thinks about the dog, is it kusala or akusala sīla?

Is it useful to feel sad? Is it all taken for oneself and "my difficult situation"? Akusala thinking does not bring any benefit and it is accumulated. We may think about the dog's feeling but what about one's own citta now? The best way is always the moment of kusala which makes it possible to help in the right way. We may try to help the dog not to have pain, but we cannot know the dog's citta. We cannot know whether it has akusala kamma which will condition birth in hell or kusala kamma which will condition birth in heaven. However we help, it depends on past kamma and the accumulations of the dog as to what the result will be.

In truth there is no dog, no "you", no friend. There are just different realities. Paññā has to develop to understand what is kusala or akusala. The best way is to help with less akusala, such as feeling sad. Understanding leads to all kinds of wholesome manners and behaviour in any situation.

So just do your best with wholesome cittas, such as speaking with kindness and understanding.

For the arahat who is fully enlightened, there is no more kusala or akusala sīla. Instead there are kiriya (inoperative) cittas which bring no results. There will be no new life.

> When a man possesses ten qualities, carpenter, I describe him as accomplished in what is wholesome, perfected in what is wholesome, an ascetic invincible attained to the supreme attainment.
>
> [But first of all] I say, it must be understood thus: 'These are unwholesome habits (akusalā sīlā),' and thus: 'Unwholesome habits originate from this,' and thus: 'Unwholesome habits cease without remainder here,' and thus: 'One practising in this way is practising the way to the cessation of unwholesome habits.'

> *And I say, it must be understood thus: 'These are wholesome habits (kusalā sīlā)', and thus: 'Wholesome habits originate from this,' and thus: 'Wholesome habits cease without remainder here,' and thus: 'One practising in this way is practising the way to the cessation of wholesome habits.'*
>
> Majjhima Nikāya 78, Samaṇamaṇḍika Sutta (Translated by Bhikkhu Ñāṇamoli and Bhikkhu Bodhi)

118

Troubles in the World

Yuan and other friends brought up the topic of troubles in the world, such as "Covid" and wars. What could the Buddha's Teachings do to help?

The way taught by the Buddha is to understand the truth of whatever is real now, no matter the circumstances.

We hear about Covid but is there any understanding now? Death can come at any time. Whatever appeared in this life before has gone. What is there now?

If we do not wish to understand the truth, we will have trouble all the time, thinking of one situation after another. However, when there is understanding, there is no trouble. There is no need to think about all these issues, it is just thinking with clinging, aversion and ignorance most of the time. It is a relief when there is understanding at any time.

There is always thinking about oneself and this or that situation when actually there is no "I", no situation, such as a war, in reality. There are just different realities arising by conditions. The more clinging there is, the more trouble there must be thinking about all the various concerns in the world.

In truth, no one can do anything. There is just seeing, hearing, smelling, tasting, touching and thinking. Why keep thinking on and on about Covid or the war, just creating more disturbance and trouble?

When there is seeing now, where is Covid? What kind of citta is thinking about it? Is it attachment, aversion or perhaps understanding that it is just a reality which has gone immediately? Temporary death is right now at each moment, so why fear death from Covid or war or anything else? What arose a moment ago has already completely gone.

Whatever seems to be the trouble is just unwholesome thinking. The disease of the mind is more fearful than the disease of he body. Does anyone see the danger of ignorance which conditions all kinds of unwholesomeness? We have fear of so many things, such as disease, death and wars, but no fear of ignorance. It is time not to be fearful of anything because of understanding the truth.

Khun Neelapa mentioned she experiences a lot of physical pain which makes it difficult for her to sleep. When there is no understanding, there is always the idea of something belonging to me or someone - it is "my pain" or "your pain". Whatever we read about in the Tipiṭaka is just about daily life. It is all about ignorance, attachment and aversion causing trouble all the time.

This very moment is the only moment that what is real can be understood. Such understanding is the only way not to be troubled by whatever one thinks about. It is not easy, but the understanding develops little by little, naturally, in daily life.

> *Bhikkhu, as to the source through which perceptions and notions [born of] mental proliferation beset a man: if nothing is found there to delight in, welcome and hold to, this is the end of the underlying tendency to lust, of the underlying tendency to aversion, of the underlying tendency to views, of the underlying tendency to doubt, of the underlying tendency to conceit, of the underlying tendency to desire for being, of the underlying tendency to ignorance; this is the end of resorting to rods and weapons, of quarrels, brawls, disputes, recrimi-*

nation, malicious words, and false speech; here these evil unwholesome states cease without remainder.

Majjhima Nikāya 18, The Honeyball (Translated by Bhikkhu Ñāṇamoli and Bhikkhu Bodhi)

119

Forgetfulness

Lukas brought up the topic of being forgetful and lack of awareness. Ann also brought up the topic of lapses of memory.

At each moment, saññā (memory) arises and marks and remembers whatever is experienced. However, when we want to think about something else, there is clinging, often with the idea of a self. That is why we say "I forget". When there is the remembering of what one likes or does not like, it is by conditions. There is still the idea of "I" as long as there is not enough understanding.

What one is thinking or talking about now is according to one's accumulations and, in particular, to vitakka cetasika, the mental factor which 'touches' the object. It arises at each moment in the day other than with moments of seeing, hearing, smelling, tasting and bodily experiencing.

> *Lukas:* I'm lazy and forgetful all day. The Buddha said not to be lazy.
>
> *Ajahn Sujin:* There are different cittas and cetasikas all day, different realities which are not to be taken for self. Understand each one clearly so there is less taking them for self.
>
> What about seeing now when you don't think about forgetting whatever appears? If you think about other things there is no understanding of what appears now. It's impossible. There is no one, just different cittas and cetasikas. Don't mind about what has gone, otherwise

> there is just clinging to that which will never return at all. There is just the wanting to have this or that experience but not understanding that moment as not "I". Forgetfulness is real. Remembrance is real. There are just different realities. Whatever arises is conditioned to be just as it is. With no understanding there is just more craving and wishing.
>
> Each word should be studied very carefully to bring firm confidence in the truth at this moment. Whatever arises is gone. It's useless to think about it because it's gone. When there is not enough understanding there must be forgetfulness because the intellectual understanding is not firm enough.

Paññā cetasika can only understand what appears now by conditions. This understanding is the only way to eliminate desire and attachment to the idea of a self. We think about other things, about this and that, but what about seeing now? However little understanding there is does not matter. The strong defilements have been accumulated for aeons and aeons. How can they be eradicated so soon? It is impossible.

When we think about weak memory, it is a conventional way of looking at the difficulty. Saññā always arises and performs its function. The goal is not to try to understand or remember other things but to develop a little more understanding. What arises now is seeing, hearing, what is seen, what is heard or thinking, for example. Usually there is not enough understanding to let go of the idea of self or something with regard to these realities. What is the absolute truth of what appears now? Seeing now is not "my seeing" or any thing. The same applies to what is seen. This is the real world now. Saññā marks and remembers what is experienced but it conditions the thinking about what is taken for the world such as people and things. There can be the letting go of the idea of doing something.

Instead there can be the gradual development of understanding with firm confidence of the truth.

> *When, bhikkhus, a carpenter or a carpenter's apprentice looks at the handle of his adze, he sees the impressions of his fingers and his thumb, but he does not know: 'So much of the adze handle has been worn away today, so much yesterday, so much earlier.' But when it has worn away, the knowledge occurs to him that it has worn away.*
>
> *So too, bhikkhus, when a bhikkhu dwells devoted to development, even though no such knowledge occurs to him: 'So much of my taints has been worn away today, so much yesterday, so much earlier,' yet when they are worn away, the knowledge occurs to him that they have been worn away.*
>
> Saṃyutta Nikāya 22:101, The Adze Handle (Translated by Bhikkhu Bodhi)

120

Calm

Vietnamese friends brought up the topic of the development of calmness. The citta and cetasikas are calmed down at all moments of kusala. However, even if the calm is highly developed and leads to various jhānas, it is said to be the wrong path (micchā paṭipadā). This is because, even though it is very calm, it is not the path to enlightenment (sammā paṭipadā) because it does not lead to the cessation of ignorance and attachment.

If one does not study the teachings carefully one may take that calmness for the understanding of the truth. This will not happen when there is the right understanding of realities, because then there is no wish to develop calmness to jhāna or have any special experience.

Some people in the Buddha's time naturally developed calmness to jhāna along with right understanding of the path, so he taught for these people too. There were various kinds of followers according to different accumulations. There were those who had previously attained jhāna and now developed insight. There were many more "sukha vipassaka" (dry insight attainers) who became enlightened without (mundane) jhāna than those who attained jhāna which had become the basis for their enlightenment.

The accumulations cannot be known until they arise when understanding the truth. Even now there are different accumulations for all of us. Who can tell what they are for the others? It is impossible. Only right understanding can know how different tendencies can arise unexpectedly.

"The truth is so very close!", as Ajahn Sujin says.

In the quote below, the Buddha is comparing the micchā paṭipadā with the sammā paṭipadā.

The commentary makes it clear that any states which do not lead out of saṃsāra are included in the wrong path. These include meritorious deeds (puññābhisaṅkhāra), even arūpa jhāna states (āneñjābhisaṅkhāra). This wrong path prolongs the cycle of rebirth.

The right path is the development of satipaṭṭhāna and insight, leading to the eradication of ignorance and craving and the cycle of rebirth.

> At Sāvatthi. 'Bhikkhus, I will teach you the wrong way and the right way. Listen to that and attend closely, I will speak.'
>
> 'Yes, venerable sir,' those bhikkhus replied. The Blessed One said this:
>
> 'And what, bhikkhus, is the wrong way? With ignorance as condition, volitional formations [come to be]; with volitional formations as condition, consciousness... Such is the origin of this whole mass of suffering. This, bhikkhus, is called the wrong way.'
>
> 'And what, bhikkhus, is the right way? With the remainderless fading away and cessation of ignorance

comes cessation of volitional formations; with the cessation of volitional formations, cessation of consciousness... Such is the cessation of this whole mass of suffering. This, bhikkhus, is called the right way.'

Saṃyutta Nikāya 12:3, The Two Ways (Translated by Bhikkhu Bodhi)

121

Sakkāya Diṭṭhi

Vietnamese friends brought up the topic of the twenty kinds of sakkāya diṭṭhi (wrong view of self) and asked for examples.

These kinds of sakkāya diṭṭhi refer to how each of the khandhas (the various rūpas and nāmas) are taken for oneself, belonging to oneself, within oneself or outside oneself. When the khandhas are taken for oneself or for others, other wrong views follow. All wrong views stem from different kinds of sakkāya diṭṭhi, the wrong ideas about oneself.

> *Ajahn Sujin:* Is that which appears now permanent? When it doesn't appear as permanent (or lasting) can there be the idea of something or someone there?

For example, does it seem that there is a finger that is typing that is a part of one's body? This would be the idea of something appearing as lasting or permanent, a kind of sakkāya diṭṭhi. When there is no understanding of the reality experienced, such as hardness or visible object, but there is the idea that something is still there, it cannot be right.

The idea of something or someone existing is deeply rooted. It is not a matter of counting how many kinds of sakkāya and other kinds of wrong view there are.

If there were not the five khandhas they could not be taken for something and for a self in different ways. For example, when we wonder where the self is or think it is in the body, it shows there is the idea that "I'm there!". When seeing is taken for one's own seeing or one wonders where it is, there is the idea of a self.

It can be known, however, that these realities are just dhammas arising by conditions and then gone forever. They have to be understood directly as they are, one by one, otherwise they are bound to be taken for a self or for something again and again. The truth is not far away but without clear understanding of what is experienced now, it is covered up by ideas of shapes, forms and something lasting.

There may be the idea that "I" see now, the seeing is "I", or the seeing belongs to "me". With understanding it can be known now which kind of sakkāya diṭṭhi it is, but there is no need to try and find out otherwise it hinders the right understanding developing naturally. Understanding the truth that seeing sees, not a self, is much more precious.

> As to the various views that arise in the world, householder, 'The world is eternal' or 'The world is not eternal'; or 'The world is finite' or 'The world is infinite'; or 'The soul and the body are the same' or 'The soul is one thing, the body is another'; or 'The Tathāgata exists after death,' or 'The Tathāgata does not exist after death,' or 'The Tathāgata both exists and does not exist after death,' or 'The Tathāgata neither exists nor does not exist after death'- these as well as the sixty two speculative views mentioned in the Brahmajāla: when there is identity view, these views come to be; when there is no identity view, these views do not come to be.
>
> Saṃyutta Nikāya 41:3, Isidatta (Translated by Bhikkhu Bodhi)

122

The Drunken Driver

We discussed Da Zhuang's story about someone walking down a street and being hit by a drunken driver. Is the injury or death the result of the negligence of the driver or of the prior akusala kamma of the victim?

If there is no understanding of what appears now, there is thinking and more and more questions about this and that situation or issue. Instead of thinking about someone being hit by a drunk driver, what about understanding seeing now or what is seen now?

What is there at this moment or any other moment? There are just experiences through six doorways. For example, there are moments of seeing what is visible, moments of experiencing what is tangible through the body-sense and moments of thinking about ideas. It is not just a matter of understanding the meaning of words such as kamma and vipāka but of understanding at this very moment that these realities do not belong to anyone.

The truth of realities is so subtle that it takes time to understand the characteristic of one reality at a time. Thinking of someone hitting or being hit is not the understanding of realities at all. At this moment of seeing is there anyone who sees? If realities are not understood as not belonging to a self, there is more and more thinking about people, cars and accidents because of memory conditioning the ignorant thinking about such events.

So usually there is ignorance of the truth that there are just dhammas arising and falling away instantly. Death may come at any moment. Before that, will there be any understanding of the truth?

The birth consciousness of the present life was the result of past kamma from a previous life, but that kamma also produces many more moments of resultant consciousness in the present life. These include the moments of seeing, hearing, smelling, tasting and bodily experiencing.

Da Zhuang wondered whether one can change the world or improve the situation.

A person cannot change anything, but understanding can condition wholesome qualities such as kindness and tolerance, no matter what occurs. There can be friendliness to the drunken driver or the victim. There can be understanding of what is true.

So to help the world, understand what is there - no one at all!

> Then the Venerable Ānanda approached the Blessed One... and said to him: "Venerable sir, it is said, 'Empty is the world, empty is the world.' In what way, venerable sir, is it said, 'Empty is the world'?"
> "It is, Ānanda, because it is empty of self and of what belongs to self that it is said, 'Empty is the world.'
> "And what is empty of self and of what belongs to self?
> "The eye, Ānanda, is empty of self and of what belongs to self. Forms are empty of self and of what belongs to self. Eye-consciousness is empty of self and of what belongs to self. Eye-contact is empty of self and of what belongs to self... Whatever feeling arises with mind-contact as condition — whether pleasant or painful or neither-painful-nor-pleasant — that too is empty of self and of what belongs to self.
> "It is, Ānanda, because it is empty of self and of what belongs to self that it is said, 'Empty is the world'."
>
> Saṃyutta Nikāya 35:85, Empty is the World (Translated by Bhikkhu Bodhi)

123

The Body

Body-sense is a rūpa, bodily element (kāya dhātu) arising and falling away all over the body. Without body-sense as doorway, the tangible objects (heat/cold, hardness/softness and motion) could not be experienced by body consciousness.

Nina mentioned that it's difficult to let go of the clinging to the idea of a body existing. Even when hearing there is "no one" or "no body" it is not understood, but the understanding has to develop.

Ajahn Sujin: And it's time to understand whether there is "I" or not all over "my body". Is there a body now in truth?

Nina: Difficult.

Ajahn Sujin: Is there anyone's body? The hardness is just the object of experiencing. In truth there is nothing, only one object being experienced at a time.

Does it belong to anyone? Is it my body or my hand? Not at all, it's only hardness appearing. In truth it cannot be anything. Now it's not appearing as it is because it seems to be my body when in truth it's only hardness.

The various concepts, such as the body, bird, cat or my hand, are all taken to be real. In truth there are only different rūpas arising and falling away that are taken for "my body". The understanding has to develop until it is very firm.

> **In this body, apart from the above mentioned collection (of primary and derived materiality), there is no body, man, woman or anything else. Beings engender wrong belief, in many ways, in the bare groups of things mentioned above. Therefore the men of old said:**
>
>> **What he sees that is not (properly) seen;**
>> **What is seen, that he does not (properly) see;**
>> **Not seeing (properly) he is shackled clean;**
>> **And he, the shackled fool, cannot get free.**
>
> **'Not seeing properly he is shackled' [means] Not seeing with the eye of wisdom this body as it actually is, he thinks: 'This is mine, this am I, this is my self,' and is bound with the fetter of defilement.**
>
> Commentary to Majjhima Nikāya 10, Satipaṭṭhāna Sutta (Translated by Soma Thera)

124

Relax, it's Gone!

Maeve introduced the topic of planning and control.

When there is firm confidence that whatever arises is conditioned at any time and place, it becomes apparent that there is no one who makes plans. The reality arising now cannot be changed or controlled by an imaginary self. It can only exist by conditions.

Ajahn Sujin: No regrets, no expectations!.

In other words, the understanding has to develop that there is no one at all. What arises does so by conditions so it is useless to have regrets about what occurred in the past or expectations about what will occur in future. No matter whether wholesome or unwholesome realities arise, they are all conditioned.

AS: Relax, it's gone!

The next moment can be a moment of understanding the truth. It all depends on condtions. Even thinking now is conditioned. Whatever arises pops up by conditions and is gone instantly. When there is clear understanding that whatever arises pops up in this way, there is no thinking of "I" doing anything, no "I" planning or controlling anything. There is no one there at all.

AS: Paññā knows!

No one does anything, but there can be understanding of the way life is. It must be the way it is!

> The vile (kucchita) that is done (kata) is villainy (kukata). The state of that is worry (kukucca). It has subsequent regret as its characteristic. Its function is to sorrow about what has and what has not been done. It is manifested as remorse. Its proximate cause is what

has and what has not been done. It should be regarded as slavery.

Visuddhimagga XIV, 174 (Translated by Bhikkhu Ñāṇamoli)

Glossary

adhi higher
ajjhattika internal
akusala unwholesome
anāgāmī non-returner, the noble person who has realized the third stage of enlightenment
anantara paccaya proximity condition
anattā non self
anicca impermanent
anubyañjana signs and details (of realities)
anusaya latent tendency
arahant noble person who has attained the fourth and final stage of enlightenment
ārakkhā protection
ārammaṇa the object of consciousness
ariya noble, the person who has attained enlightenment
āsava canker, intoxicant, subtle defilement
avijjā ignorance
avyākata dhammas (realities) which are not kusala or akusala
āyatana meeting dhamma
āyūhana kamma at birth which brings results during a lifetime.
bāhira external
bhāvanā mental development, the development of calm, samatha, and the development of insight, vipassanā.
bhāvanā-māya-paññā understanding based on mental development

bhavaṅga citta life-continuum citta
bhavāsava the āsava that is clinging to becoming

bhikkhu monk
cetanā intention or volition (a cetasika)
cetasika mental factor arising with consciousness
chanda interest (a cetasika)
citta consciousness, the chief reality which experiences an object
cittā-maya-paññā understanding based on wise considering
cittānupassanā awareness and understanding of citta
cuti-citta death consciousness
dāna generosity, giving
dhamma reality, the natural law, the Teaching of The Buddha
dhātu element, any reality
diṭṭhi wrong view
dosa aversion or ill-will (a cetasika)
dukkha unsatisfactoriness
gocara object or field
hadaya-vatthu heart-base
hetu root
iddhi spiritual power
iddhi-pāda base for spiritual power leading to enlightenment
indriya faculty, leader
javana impulsion (function of cittas) which "run through" the object
jhāna absorption, burning, developed in samatha or vipassanā
kalāpa group (e.g., group of rūpas)
kamma intention or volition; cetana cetasika
kāya collection, body of rūpas or mental body, the cetasikas
kāya-dhātu body-sense element
khandha one of a group, any conditioned reality, i.e. any rūpa, vedanā, saññā, sankhāra or viññāna

kiriya citta inoperative citta which is not kusala, akusala or vipāka
kusala wholesome
lobha attachment (a cetasika)
lobha-mūla-citta citta rooted in attachment
loka world, dhamma which arises and falls away
magga path, Eightfold Path
māna conceit (a cetasika)
manasikāra attention (a cetasika)
Māra the evil one
mettā loving kindness
micchā wrong
moha ignorance (a cetasika)
nāma any reality which can experience an object
ñāṇa understanding, wisdom
nibbāna the unconditioned reality which is freedom from dukkha
nimitta mental image or sign
paccaya condition
pāda basis
paṇḍara pure, clear
paññā wisdom or understanding
paññatti concept which makes known
paramattha dhamma absolute, ultimate reality
pāramī perfection, 10
pariññā understanding between stages of insight
pariyatti intellectual right understanding of reality
paṭicca samuppāda dependent origination
paṭipadā path
paṭipatti direct understanding of reality, lit. reaching the particular (object)

paṭisandhi citta rebirth consciousness

phassa contact (a cetasika)

rūpa physical reality which cannot experience anything

sacca truth

sakkāya-diṭṭhi wrong view of self

samādhi concentration or one-pointedness

samanantara paccaya contiguity condition

samatha calm

sammā right

saṃsāra cycle of existence

saṅkappa vitakka cetasika

saṅkhāra dhamma conditioned reality

saṅkhārakkhandha all cetasikas other than vedanā (feeling) and saññā (memory)

saññā perception or memory

sati awareness (a cetasika)

satipaṭṭhāna awareness of a reality. It can be the cetasika sati or the object of mindfulness

sīla morality, behaviour of cittas

sīlabbataparāmāsa adherence to rites and rituals

sotāpanna noble person who has attained the first stage of enlightenment

sukhavipassaka with dry insight

suññatā mpty of self

suta-maya-paññā understanding based on hearing

Tathāgata "Thus-gone", The Buddha

Theravāda Teaching of the Elders

uddhacca restlessness (a cetasika)

upādā rūpa derived rūpa, any rūpa other than the four great elements

upādāna clinging

upādānakkhandha any khandha which is the object of clinging.

upanibhandha anchoring with direct understanding

upanissaya decisive support, habitual

vedanā feeling (a cetasika)

viññāṇa consciousness vipāka citta (and cetasikas) which are the result of kamma.

vipassanā insight, wisdom which sees realities as they are

viriya energy, effort, patience (a cetasika)

vitakka striking, directs the citta to the object (a cetasika)

yoniso manasikāra wise attention

Biography

Sarah Procter Abbott has been studying and sharing the Buddha's teachings as preserved in the Theravadin (or Pali language) tradition for over 45 years, under the continuous guidance of the Thai Buddhist teacher Ajahn Sujin Boriharnwanaket. During this time she helped share the Dhamma in England, Hong Kong, Australia, Vietnam, Taiwan, Thailand, Sri Lanka and other countries. For the past 20 years she and her husband Jonothan have hosted an internet Buddhist discussion group, Dhamma Study Group. It currently has 1000 members and an archive of 170,000 messages. Sarah and Jonothan lived in Hong Kong for 40 years, until moving to Sydney recently. Sarah worked as a psychologist and teacher.

Further Study

- The Dhamma Study and Support Foundation
  www.dhammahome.com/en
- Dhamma Study Group
  A discussion forum for anyone interested in understanding the Buddha's teachings.
  groups.io/g/dsg
- Zolag – Books on Buddhism
  www.zolag.co.uk

www.ingramcontent.com/pod-product-compliance
Lightning Source LLC
Chambersburg PA
CBHW022120040426
42450CB00006B/782